MINDFULLY WISE
LEADERSHIP

MINDFULLY WISE LEADERSHIP

THE SECRET
OF TODAY'S LEADERS

Keren Tsuk, PhD

ROWMAN & LITTLEFIELD
Lanham • Boulder • New York • London

Published by Rowman & Littlefield
An imprint of The Rowman & Littlefield Publishing Group, Inc.
4501 Forbes Boulevard, Suite 200, Lanham, Maryland 20706
www.rowman.com

86-90 Paul Street, London EC2A 4NE, United Kingdom

British Library Cataloguing in Publication Information Available

Library of Congress Cataloging-in-Publication Data Available

ISBN: 978-1-5381-5636-0 (cloth : alk. paper)
ISBN: 978-1-5381-5637-7 (electronic)

CONTENTS

FOREWORD

A few years ago, I was visiting my mother in rural Kansas, where I grew up. For entertainment we went to a local antiques shop. Among the dusty relics was a stack of old *Time* and *Life* magazines. I searched the pile for some samples from my birth year, 1969. I wanted to see what the consciousness was like when I entered the world. I found a world with different sensitivities than our current lives about fifty years later. There were advertisements for sugar—proudly described by the Sugar Growers Association as "The Natural Energy Source." There were advertisements for cigarettes pitched by medical doctors, encouraging us to light up for our health. There were articles that talked about race and gender in ways that would surely make us cringe today. In many ways we've evolved over the past fifty years.

Amid that consciousness, there was an article about a midwestern university swim team. They had been successful, and the reporter was digging in to learn more. The headline shouted, "Athletes Subject Themselves to Self-torture in Order to Win." I wondered what in the world they were doing. My mind raced. Electroshock therapy? Ice baths? Nope. Do you know what extreme measures these young men were taking? They were lifting weights! In 1969 strength training was new. It was strange, foreign. Also, it was highly effective. Since it was highly effective, other swim teams wanted to know more. Fast-forward fifty years. Today, pretty much everyone knows the benefits of exercise. We know the benefits of strength training. Not everyone does it, but we all know it's good for us.

Mindfulness, meditation, and other "mental" exercises are on a similar journey to the mainstream as physical exercise. There are now more than six thousand peer-reviewed papers that catalog the benefits of mindfulness: better sleep, lessened effects of physical stress, better quality of relationships, more focus, more resilience, increased creativity. The list goes on. Apps like Headspace, Calm, and Insight Timer are becoming more and more popular with individuals looking to become a better version of themselves.

Many companies are taking notice. They are starting to offer programs for employees as part of their corporate wellness offerings. Employers know that a happy and resilient employee is good for business.

There are still hurdles to get over. Just like strength training in 1969 was new and strange, some view mindfulness through the same lens. There are many misconceptions about mindfulness. Is it the same as meditation? Is it religious? Will others think I'm strange? What does meditating have to do with work? Beyond these doubts, we're seeing the proof. Study after study highlights the benefits of a regular practice. More leaders are sharing their personal stories of transformation.

We're still in the early days of bringing mindfulness, and hopefully compassion, into our workplace, but it's coming, surely and undeniably. Individuals are becoming increasingly familiar with mindfulness. Leaders are becoming increasingly comfortable speaking openly about their practices. Companies are slowly realizing that making meditation and mindfulness offerings available to their employees is good for everyone.

Just as physical exercise, including strength training, has made the leap from new and strange to mainstream and commonplace, mindfulness is on its way to the mainstream. Companies that value their employees' well-being will make these offerings available. All individuals will understand the benefits that mindfulness offers. Not everyone will do it, but the opportunity will be there.

This time, it won't take fifty years to make the transition.

Scott Shute
Head of Mindfulness and Compassion Programs, LinkedIn

INTRODUCTION

When I completed my PhD, I realized that I wanted to shift my research into a public forum. Writing a book would fulfill my desire to make knowledge about mindful leadership accessible and easy to implement.

I remember that in the process of writing my dissertation, after going through the committee and getting approved for the research proposal, I had reached the stage of searching for an organization where I could conduct the research. I was sure this was the easy stage in the research, but that proved not to be the case.

At the time, a friend, who is also a colleague, reminded me that he worked as a consultant at a technology company with a meditation room. I called the Human Resources manager of that company, and she referred me to the CEO. At the meeting I told the CEO about the study and its topic. He said that he meditated personally and had built a suitable room where he could both meditate and share his experience with others. He also said he believed that people should enjoy working.

When I said I was an organizational consultant and that I could help them, he replied that they had consultants working with the company and that he was asking himself how he could help me.

His approach surprised me.

The managers in other companies I had under consideration merely wanted to know what was in it for them. One of those managers even asked me to issue a summary report stating these benefits.

This CEO, on the other hand, wanted to help me. He was giving for the sake of giving. It was a feeling I had not had in meetings with other companies, and I felt blessed to find this organization and get to work.

Writing a PhD dissertation was a dream come true for me. My inner motivation was so deep that even in complex and sometimes discouraging moments, I did not think for a moment that stopping was an option. I even remember the moment the call came from the university to tell me my doctorate had been approved. This is one of the defining moments of my life, and I will never forget it. We were all at home, my husband, Sharon, and my two children; Reuti was about six months old, and Yoavi, my elder son, was about five years old. The phone rang, and when I picked it up and heard the news, I felt that I had won the lottery. I ended the call and released a long-awaited shout of joy.

I was so happy that I put on music and started dancing and jumping with my kids. Yoavi was thrilled that his mother was dancing and going wild. He stopped dancing and asked, "Mama, why are you so happy?" I told him, "Yoavi, this is how you feel when dreams come true."

So, what is my dream?

My dream is to create a situation where organizations are a platform for humanity's development. While that might sound pretentious, it is my vision, and I believe in it with all my heart. I aspire that organizations will allow their employees to develop and grow and to fulfill themselves. I hope to see jobs that serve employees, customers, and the environment, and companies that operate from a win-win paradigm of profit for all and a great purpose. I believe with all my heart that this is the change we, as humanity, need to go through. We must move from a place of alienation, exploitation, and separation to a state of unity, service, attentiveness, and harmony among people, between people and the environment, and among organizational activities so that optimal work will be done to enable prosperity and growth.

Mindful leadership enables us, as managers, to be mindful to ourselves, employees, customers, and the changing market needs—and from this place create workplaces that engage talented people and enable them to thrive, be creative, and innovate.

As I see it, the more we work out of mindfulness to ourselves and to others, the more sustainable workplaces will be created, ones that will enable better connections between people, enhance the flow experience at work, allow us to put in the least effort, and maximize results with a sense of belonging and meaningfulness.

As we increase our mindfulness in our day-to-day routine, we will be able to handle changing and challenging situations in a better manner by being able to pause and be present with the uncertainty and the discomfort. And from this place, new creative and innovative solutions will emerge—solutions that are not a reconstruction of the past but a flash of the new.

Even so, you are probably asking yourself: *Why should I read this book and embrace the principles it offers?*

We live in a hectic reality and an intriguingly extraordinary period, and we find ourselves perpetually challenged. We are in the midst of a transformation; the Coronavirus pandemic is transforming the way we live as well as the economic and business world.

As managers who want to run successful, creative, and innovative organizations, we need to be flexible in our thinking and be able to rapidly adjust and adopt new tools to motivate our organizations to be at the cutting edge; mindfulness allows that to take place.

More than ever before, we need mindful leadership.

1

LANDMARKING LEADERSHIP

Tantalus Financial Group decided to hold a bicycle day. (*Note:* Tantalus is a pseudonym for a real company in Israel, as are the names of its employees discussed in this book.)

It was a simple call to action for the company. To raise public awareness about air pollution, Tantalus's employees would ride bicycles to high-tech companies and hand out leaflets encouraging cycling to work at least once a month.

The evening before the event, however, Jaden, the company's founder, sent an email to his employees explaining that he had to fly to Asia at the last minute and couldn't make the event. He attached a photo of himself wearing a branded event cycling shirt.

The response was cynical. There was resistance among employees, focusing on the disconnect between the image the company was trying to present and the founder's actual conduct. Despite the rhetoric about the importance of contributing to the community, once a business need clashed with social responsibility, the business need took precedence. Employees expressed their displeasure by hanging a sign on the bulletin board with an image of Jaden wearing the bicycle day shirt, with the caption, "Bike every day." Next to the caption the employees wrote, "Except today."

This pervasive cynicism had emerged because quite a few employees weren't on board with management's ambition to increase awareness regarding the environment, at least in the way management had imagined it would all roll out. Employees cited the difficulty of connecting and getting other tech workers on board without sharing their thinking, without testing their interest, and the company's choice of donation channels associated with the event.

Management soon convened a company meeting to discuss the matter. Michael, the CEO, explained that despite several ideas for community engagement on the table, he intended to target the environment because it seemed a relatable opportunity for Tantalus.

Jaden agreed. "I was looking for a message that I want to leave as a legacy. From the day I founded Tantalus, I tried to build a slightly different, pleasant, and fun place to work. We didn't always succeed. The truth is, I was personally disappointed by the team's reaction."

Michael stepped in. "This wasn't a PR scheme," he said. "We thought it would be a means to attract and retain quality people. I'd love to get feedback, questions."

Ben, a senior employee, stood up and looked around the room. "I feel that Jaden is talking about setting up a place that would be fun—a positive and forward-thinking place—for those who work there," he said. "Unfortunately, one of the side effects of engaging people is the fact that people have opinions."

According to a 2017 Gallup poll, 28 percent of respondents rated business executive honesty and ethical standards as low or very low, 54 percent rated them as average, and just 16 percent rated executives' honesty and ethics as high or very high.[1] Research over the past five years indicates that cynicism is on the rise in American business and industry, which increasingly hurts their competitiveness and ability to accommodate today's needed organizational change. Paul J. Rosen, president of the American Institute of Stress, indicates that recent, dizzying changes in technology and the economy are causing unprecedented burnout, cynicism, sickness, and absenteeism.[2] That's why organizational cynicism is widespread among organizations globally.[3]

A lack of trust and honesty creates cynicism. Organizational cynicism is a feeling of dissatisfaction toward the organization when employees believe that management lacks honesty, justice, and transparency. Cynicism is an intrinsic distrust of the intentions of others, a belief that others are not representing their true motives. This includes a negative attitude and aggravation toward the organization. It is a sign that people are feeling hopeless and powerless. They may feel unsafe, devalued, not listened to. They may see leaders as being ineffective or as not having their best interests at heart. And they have no faith that the organization will ever change things for the better. Employees are cynical when they feel they are being used merely to achieve goals, without really being seen, and when they feel a gap between what managers say and how they act. This causes people to emotionally disengage—and yet they often stay with the company, sometimes because they feel they have few other choices.

This cynicism in the workplace is like poison. It is contagious, and it can prevent employees from engaging, connecting with one another, enjoying the work, and being innovative and productive. And surely it will prevent a culture of trust—the essence of creative and innovative companies.

At Tantalus, employees were cynical. This was especially the case when they perceived a gap between what management stated were the organization's values and the way people were expected to act. They aren't alone. At many companies, leaders make decisions without consulting key employee experts; therefore, timelines and projects are often stalled. Employees feel emotionally disengaged, and yet they stay at the organization because of challenges in the job market. This cynicism in the workplace is contagious and prevents effective work, engagement, and innovation.

These challenges prevent a culture of trust from forming. People want to feel that they have an impact, and they need power and freedom of action to make this work. Authority needs to be based on the leader's ability to make connections with, persuade, and motivate others. In many companies, leaders make an effort to invite employees to speak authentically, yet feelings of stress and anxiety prevent needed self-awareness, empathy, vulnerability, and an openness to moving forward in the organization.

In this case, what is clearly lacking between the leadership team and the rest of the company is trust. The company is employing a hierarchical form of leadership, but leaders are telling the rest of the company that they have a flat structure. This feels dishonest, as if the organization is incapable of telling their employees the truth about how things really work. Employees feel that they are being gaslighted—they are told that their opinions are valued while, at the same time, those opinions are ignored.

If not addressed, this kind of situation can become a crisis for both a leader and an organization.

THE PERPETUAL CHALLENGE MACHINE

In the modern business world, we live in a hectic reality but also in an intriguingly extraordinary period; we find ourselves perpetually challenged. We're being pushed to work toward social equity in business, and we recognize the impact of our work on the environment on a global basis. Add to this the Coronavirus pandemic that is transforming the way we live, as well as the economic and business world. We are already experiencing changes that are becoming the new normal, such as the hybrid work environment—a blended model where employees work a few days at the workplace and a few days from home. Employees will be given the flexibility to work when and where they want. Some organizations will cease to exist, while others will pop up. Many companies are having to reevaluate their business models and offerings because company leadership is now expected to coach rather than simply impose their ideas on their employees.

In fact, the statistics are dire.

We can't disconnect people from work. Think about where we spend most of our time. In a given week in North America, most of us spend an average of forty-seven hours at work. We also spend an average of seven hours a week commuting, more in major centers. That's roughly 56 out of 112 waking hours that we spend directly engaged with our jobs, and that allocation of time dedicated to work is only increasing.[4] That's half our lives either at or traveling to and from work. Workdays are getting longer for all of us. Work is also intensifying. Consider this disturbing survey result from the 2019 Gallup Workplace Poll: Fifty-eight percent of people said they trust strangers more than they do their own boss. The same poll tells us that 85 percent of employees either are not engaged or are actively disengaged at work. The economic consequences of this are approximately *seven trillion* dollars in lost productivity. New research from the field shows the demands on our time in the office increasing, while surveillance of our day-to-day tasks is also on the rise. The level of mental effort and strain we experience is consistently undermeasured by companies.[5] That may be why, according to Deloitte's most recent employee survey, 71 percent of people in North America would walk right out the door and take a new job tomorrow if they were offered one.

Especially in today's new normal, as shown in a March 2021 Microsoft study, high productivity is masking an exhausted workforce.[6] Self-assessed productivity has remained the same or higher for many employees over the past year, but at a human cost. Nearly one in five global survey respondents say their employer doesn't care about their work-life balance, 45 percent feel overworked, and 39 percent feel exhausted. The digital intensity of workers' days has increased substantially, with the average number of meetings and chats steadily rising since last year.

This kind of workplace stress can result in extreme employee reactions, the kind that suggest that employees are already halfway out the door.

According to a 2019 research survey by the US Bureau of Labor Statistics, the 2018 US annual average absence rate was 2.9 percent; unscheduled absenteeism costs were roughly $3,600 per year for each hourly worker and $2,660 each year for salaried employees—a 3.4 percent increase over the previous year.[7] In addition, aggression, hatred, and horizontal violence are seen to be increasing in the workplace because of stress, especially in fields like health care.[8] There are organizational structural characteristics that either permit or decrease the risk of violence, and these can have an impact on employees' psychological ability to either mitigate stressors in their work environment or escalate issues. The result is twofold: Either there is a high level of absenteeism as a coping mechanism or people begin to lash out to gain the attention of those who are in positions of power and force a systemic change in the organization as a whole.[9]

As managers who want to run successful, creative, and innovative organizations, we need to be flexible in our thinking and be able to rapidly adjust and adopt new tools to motivate our organizations to be at the cutting edge.

Tantalus was right in the middle of these changes a couple of years ago.

At the time it was facing these challenges, Tantalus was a publicly traded US company with offices around the world. Founded in New York in 1987, it combined the world of high technology with the trade and stock market, providing technology solutions to companies operating in the financial field. I conducted my research at their development site in Israel. During this time, the company underwent a change with the arrival of a new CEO, Michael.

The founder and former CEO, Jaden, had been appointed president of the Israel arm of Tantalus, and was responsible for Asia Pacific regional technology development.

I was embedded at Tantalus as a part of a two-year doctoral research project that focused on the changing business dynamic for global companies that had started to explore and, later, employ mindfulness practices at work.

Since my time there, Tantalus has been acquired by another entity, but my exploration of the organization allowed me firsthand access to how this company, and others I was able to explore along the way, grappled with the deep questions of how to move into the mindfulness space. It is from this research project and others that I developed a course called Mindfulness Based Leadership to help companies increase their mindfulness experience, presence, and daily awareness—and help the bottom line. Through an analysis of what happened at Tantalus, and the hundreds of other companies I have worked with from Asia to Europe to the Middle East and beyond, I have learned just what it takes to truly practice mindfulness in a way that allows businesses to thrive.

And mindfulness is about practice.

Practice is a matter of continuous learning and improvement in which we try out different methods of skill building and dedicate different amounts of time to a range of activities that suit our personal growth as human beings. We can't simply continue to replicate "best practices," because what works for one company or person doesn't work for another, and that will continue to be the case the faster business moves over the next decade. What we *can* do is make deeper analysis and adjustments internally, intentionally.

Every time we ask a question of ourselves or others, as long as we are asking authentically rather than expecting a certain answer, we learn something; that's where the opportunity to shift comes in. Ignoring what we learn is a disservice to who we are becoming as people, to our neuroplastic development as thinkers and doers, and to what we can achieve in our organizational fellowship to create a new future. The practice shows us that every personal thought, conversation, or experience is an opportunity to make a shift. Practicing possibility thinking allows us to not worry about the future, given that we can't predict it. As we approach the future (or it is realized), all we can do is adapt, revise, and recalibrate.

STEPPING UP

A switch to mindful leadership was exactly what was unfolding in front of me at that meeting at Tantalus. Jaden and Michael were under pressure to look at the challenge in front of them, not through the lens of traditional leadership but through the eyes of their employees. They stepped up. Company management invited employees to engage in a dialogue to discuss the voices of resistance that had emerged and to create a common sense of identity and meaning. Participating employees were asked to be open and honest. They said they felt that management had used this event to promote the company's goals. They felt alienated and remote from the decision-making process.

Hearing these concerns, Jaden and Michael realized that they needed to create a space where there was room for honest and collaborative communication. They demonstrated genuine listening and expressed authentic concern and care for the opinions of Tantalus employees.

Watching them, it was evident that Jaden was fully present in the dialogue.

The ability to be present requires a degree of exposure and vulnerability; an invitation to self-reflection, learning, and changing; and the ability to examine and question our own behavior and the beliefs that have guided us. Jon Kabat-Zinn defines it as "the ability to be 'here and now' in this moment, intentionally and non-judgmentally."[10] It is a way to cope with yourself, with others, and with the world in a way that makes it possible to adopt more effective and positive ways for better behavior, behavior that is not biased by anything that has happened in the past. This is different from a situation in which we maintain and justify our power of perception, belief, and behavior without really being attentive to others and allowing their things to resonate with and change us.

Let's take the example of having a conversation with your spouse about a disagreement you have regarding the right way to act with your kids. This requires being present and listening openly to the way our spouse sees the situation in order to find the best solution for our kids—and accepting that we may need to let go of our beliefs and assumptions regarding what is the best solution. Being present and open enables a new solution to emerge.

As another example, you consider offering your client a specific solution that you think is best for them. But during the conversation, you listen deeply and come to understand that they actually need something else, not what you initially offered.

Jaden also allowed himself to be vulnerable and exposed, stating that he was personally disappointed and hurt in their reaction to the event.

Authentic emotions, which are only a small part of moving toward mindfulness at work, can facilitate spontaneous behavior, presence, and a change of identity in which team members are more able to give up their fixed opinions and perceptions. Dialogue can enable both management and employees to make room for their feelings and emotions while examining basic assumptions.

Jaden was present in the meeting, listening to the different voices around him, and he enabled these voices to change him. The change was reflected by Jaden's words after that meeting when he told me: "The employees feel it, very quickly identifying the fake, as if we were not making choices out of frank conduct. I took the lack of success or failure on a personal level."

Taking this path provided new insights into the event at Tantalus, and a range of new community engagement and charitable initiatives were considered. The team was allowed to find its own path forward, supported by Jaden and Michael, not the other way around.

Mindfulness can be nuanced and, for some, difficult to master.

As we go through the process of unpacking the operationalization of mindfulness in this book, be prepared to change the way you think about business. Be prepared to give up some of your assumptions, just like Jaden and Michael did. Through their story, and many others from the front lines of business, we'll examine just what it takes to become truly, authentically mindful, and how it's going to work in, and for, your organization.

2

THE NEW PATH
TO LEADERSHIP

Not too long ago, I led an intimate corporate retreat with only ten people. Every morning we walked up a mountain to meditate in silence; we didn't talk with one another until well after breakfast, hours later. Every day was the same: We'd ascend to the top and walk down again, and we'd take time for ourselves. On the third day, one of the corporate leaders participating in the retreat, someone who had fought his way up the ranks of a high-tech firm, had an epiphany, one that affected his next career steps. During the last meditation he was really uncomfortable sitting and had to lie down on the deck. Then it came to him. He wanted to be a teacher, not a corporate manager.

It happens, sometimes, this kind of awareness. Usually the epiphanies that arise out of a mindfulness retreat aren't so life-changing. Maybe someone realizes that what's important is for leaders to give space to employees to be a whole person in the workplace, with a range of capabilities. Maybe they begin to understand that a leader must be willing to release control so that each employee is empowered.

But change always happens—and quickly. And it's always a good thing.

Take the story of Marc Bartolini, CEO of Aetna, a major US insurance company.[1] After a serious skiing accident, he began to practice meditation and yoga. Realizing that these tools did wonders for him, he decided to bring them to the organization through online courses and research-based programs that have attracted twenty thousand employees. Eighty-seven percent of participants recommend this program to other employees, 36 percent have reported a reduction in stress, 16 percent improved their sleep, 24 percent reported improved productivity, and 18 percent experienced stress reduction.

In the real world, we're starting to see what mindful leadership looks like. Global organizations such as Aetna have been joined by LinkedIn, SAP, General Mills, Check Point, Verint, Intel, Google, Apple, Nike, Salesforce, and others to offer mindfulness programs to their employees. At Salesforce, CEO Marc Benioff presented mindfulness plans at the company's annual conference, where they offered several events that included mindful walking, conscious eating, and guided meditations. They support an annual Mindfulness Day and have opened on-site meditation rooms. SAP has also embraced mindfulness and has based their approach on the Search Inside Yourself Leadership Institute program, which originated at Google. Within six months, SAP employees experienced a 9.2 percent increase in wellness, a 6.5 percent increase in engagement, a 13.8 percent increase in focus, a total stress decrease of 7.6 percent, and increase in creativity of 12.2 percent.[2]

But despite this trend, even more companies remain in the same old paradigms we've always seen in leadership.

CONTROL DOESN'T EQUAL EFFICIENCY

The challenge is that we lean back on the assumption that traditional leadership values of the past are more likely to lead to success, even when they don't. These bureaucratic structures aimed for control based on fear in order to elicit efficiency and performance. They are the stick rather than the carrot.

Traditional leadership concepts go back a long way, connecting to the way military might was prioritized. Sun Tzu's *The Art of War* is a book many business school graduates are still forced to read. More than 2,500 years ago, the Chinese master strategist wrote about navigating through battle successfully, the first tenet of which was that you must know the enemy and yourself. Although originally meant to offer wisdom to generals, today this principle is taught to future business leaders as they sit at their desks in classrooms from Switzerland to Hong Kong to the United States as relevant to today's global business because it reads like a how-to for a multinational consumer products company: "The elements of the art of war are first, measurement of space; second, estimation of quantities; third, calculations; fourth, comparisons; and fifth, chances of victory."[3] Professors often argue that market competition is like a war, a never-ending one, and that we can use this text as a means of gathering, analyzing, synthesizing, and using information to make better decisions and take better actions on the field of play.

Business is a military hierarchy, and while leaders are supposed to be the heroes of the day, employees are expendable pawns on the front lines. It makes sense. Most of what we've created in the modern business world is a result of the post–World War II era, where we created teams on the battlefield that we moved right into the boardroom when peace broke out.

But what happens when people are pawns, when they know their interests are tertiary, their jobs precarious, their ideas subject to the hierarchy within the walls of their company? Competition. No matter how we try to sugarcoat it and tell people they are "teams of rivals" or "equals" or "peers" who mentor one another, most employees know on some level that this is not true. Not only are they required to compete against their similarly-titled associates from other firms, they must usually compete for resources, managers' time, recognition, pay, and job security inside their own firm every single day.

Employees overcompensate and overcorrect because their work journey is a solitary one. In fact, businesses are driven to worry about the fact that employees spend more than eighty minutes a week in social conversation,[4] as if this is something that should be of deep concern. Eighty minutes talking to one another per week is perceived as a bad thing. The characters that employees are asked to play run parallel to those of soldiers, disconnected from the ability to share human emotion at work, even if there are missions and value statements that superficially support teamwork. Employees are told over and over again through sports and military metaphors that they are part of a team, that they have to follow a strategic plan linked to these metaphors.

In the world of traditional leadership what was thought to motivate people was external, based on monetary rewards. We know now that this approach distanced employees and employers, creating barriers between people, businesses, and the community. Defining an executive figure by its own power was enough to harness and motivate people. Work was regarded as an effort, usually unpleasant, and people became accustomed to that.

As a result, with a lack of ethics in leadership that has been identified over and over again during challenges such as the Enron scandal and the global economic crisis, companies look for loopholes so they can make more money. They look for these loopholes because leaders' high risk–taking behaviors allow them to think they are above the law.[5] Some researchers even contend that these leaders' actions border on psychopathic because they lack any consideration for the human beings who work in their offices, factories, and global distribution chains—or their customers.

For example, even after the Sarbanes-Oxley Act was introduced after Enron management left its investors in shatters, in 2006 the State of New York was forced to sue UBS Financial Services, an international investment bank, for defrauding their customers by charging brokerage fees in the form of a percentage of assets rather than as a percentage of their investments. The case went all the way to the New York Supreme Court before the company was held liable. And companies who are already breaking the rules use their deep pockets to get free of regulations, with HSBC paying a US$1.5 billion fine in 2012 for money laundering[6] only the tip of the iceberg. The headlines are filled with similar examples, with 2020 marked by investigations into global banking practices by such behemoths as JPMorgan Chase, Standard Chartered, Deutsche Bank, and Bank of New York Mellon, as well as HSBC—again.

And that's why leadership started to change.

THE SWITCH TO SHARED LEADERSHIP

The immediate result of these ongoing challenges was a switch to what is known as "shared leadership."

A shared leadership approach to management can ease decision making; it encourages cooperation during conflicts, as it can shift the frame of reference from self-interest to the priorities of the entire organization. As it requires team members to engage in ongoing negotiation and role sharing, shared leadership supports the development of shared perceptions and aspirations for team success.[7] Under this approach, employees share and collaborate on decision making more often, thereby recognizing one another's contributions.

But there's a problem with shared leadership as well.

While the shared leadership practices of the early 2000s have allowed companies to be more open to decision making that presses for change, the focus was still on increasing organizational responsiveness to market conditions,[8] not on truly valuing the contributions of all employees.

The use of shared leadership wasn't authentic; it was a stopgap approach to *seeming* ethical in the workplace rather than *being* ethical. And this is where leadership continues to break down.

It is critical to understand that its human resources are an organization's largest group of stakeholders.

According to organizational theory, companies have the responsibility to create "joyful encounters" for their teams, encounters that are not simply a matter of following moral norms but are characterized by joyful affections that increase employees' power to act.[9] In other words, the true focus of employee engagement is to create a satisfying environment in which to work and, as noted elsewhere in the literature, to recognize that social exchange theory and equity theory have to become part of a human resource toolkit for a sustainable business.

The rationale for shifting away from traditional leadership practices that focus on the amalgamation of wealth and toward those that place emphasis on mindfulness in employee engagement is that in the new knowledge-driven economy, traditional leadership is antithetical to business success. Even within more traditional industries, it has been found that ethical business cultures that enhance employee well-being are more likely to lead to sustainable business ventures.[10] This is because positive working conditions in which mindfulness is a focus of the workplace have been shown to not only create an ethical climate or culture in organizations but also to provide a desirable work environment in other ways that further enhance followers' job performance and, at the same time, enhance business outcomes.[11]

An emphasis on mindfulness-based employee engagement leads to specific shifts in cultural norms that will lead to better performance. One of these is an overall increase in helping behaviors and group conscientiousness on the job, as opposed to the kind of internal competition that marks less-ethical business environments. Moral attentiveness can accompany these changes as well, which means there is a measured decrease in both organizational and personal deviance on the job. When people feel that they are authentically part of a team that cares about one another, they are more likely to make mindful and kind choices about their work. Cultivating these values deliberately means that employees are also more likely to show compassion, psychological flexibility, and adaptive functioning in their work tasks.

The future of business depends on creating a sustainable means of moving forward.

By sustainability, I'm not referring to dealing with the problem (and it's a big problem) of environmental issues. I mean that business has to include a focus on how we develop and embody leadership values that allow all stakeholders to thrive. It is not enough simply to make money; this only provides shareholder value and ignores the greater good—the needs of employees and suppliers and, even more so, the local and global economies in which all businesses operate and upon which all businesses' success depends. And yet, research shows that the preponderance of unethical people at leadership levels in business has led to a generalized business culture that can border on psychopathy. This in and of itself lacks any semblance of sustainability. The reality of the ways in which the world has collectively adhered to these business norms means that we have put ourselves at risk, perhaps much more so than we have realized.

The issue of ethical leadership has to be addressed through mindfulness. Companies have to take a stance that is not simply ethically-neutral. They have to be able to distinguish between leaders who always use power for self-aggrandizement and take a Machiavellian stance to governance and those who will use power for the benefit of others. Companies also need leaders who place a high emphasis on the psychological empowerment of their team members and bypass hierarchical power dynamics that result in diminishing employees. Leaders need to reinforce the use of ethical standards and lead by example so that ethics become culturally embedded in the organization.[12] This is more needed than ever in a world where diversity, equity, and inclusion have become focal areas for businesses.

But can they? Mindfulness practices at work show exactly how this is possible. And it is possible while still increasing productivity and growth.

MEANING, MINDFULNESS, AND MOTIVATION

The ability to engage employees and allow them to feel meaning and satisfaction at work happens through mindfulness. This takes place by giving space to employees' deep feelings and emotions rather than using cynical and manipulative means to use and control employees. Normative controls in traditional leadership seek to blur the boundary between the employee's self and the organization to achieve maximum commitment to the organization and identification with it.[13] Normative control encourages people to internalize high expectations and blurs the boundary between the employee's true feelings and what the company expects the employee to feel. This may create self-alienation, inauthenticity, and burnout among employees; it does not give them a sense of liberty, freedom of choice, belonging, and meaning. Control is functional and uses the employee merely as a tool for bringing profit to the organization, and employees know it is happening. It simply doesn't work.

When meaning and values begin to disappear from work, so does motivation.

Think about the example of value statements. We have our own values, ones we've built a lifetime working toward. We also see value statements on websites, in offices. This is our mission; this is what is important to us. The problem with values is that we only "value" the good things: innovation, respect, honor. We don't value being told we're wrong. We don't value learning. We don't value putting in the work. We don't always value the behaviors that lead to mindfulness, because we haven't done the hard work of self-awareness, other-awareness, and intention building. We don't value the real changes we need to make as a result of being off course in the first place. We hate being wrong. If the company values say we value "constant improvement," for example, I would suggest that we value being constantly better but not the mindful conversations required to reach true, sustained improvement.

Employees long to grow and develop both professionally and personally. This means values such as passion, meaning, vision, and a higher purpose are becoming drivers for engaging employees and motivating them to remain loyal. People are no longer willing to work at any cost at any job; jobs that reflect employees' deep inner values are highly prized and sought out. Additionally, the increasing pressure of global competition has led organizations to recognize that they increasingly face great competition for their talented employees.

Knowing all of this, a mindful leadership process should be viewed as an interactive process of influence and learning.

Whenever you learn a new skill at work, you adopt it at the pace of what's called the learning curve. It's slow at the beginning, no matter what field you are in. Newer research suggests that the learning curve can no longer be described in terms of sequential development that eventually leads to mastery, or something that can be achieved within the confines of a training program or workload. Self-beliefs and perceptions affect how the learning curve progresses: Stresses, burnout, and imposter syndrome all factor into whether this curve progresses at its normal upward rate. Job insecurity is associated with decreases in self-rated performance and the ability to adopt new information.

Allowing people, allowing ourselves, to question what we know and build on real-life practices accelerates the process. We create our own personal learning strategies when we have agency to be authentic.[14] This happens through finding meaning in our work (through learning as experience); community (through mutual engagement, joint enterprise, and shared repertoire); identity (through learning and use of shared resources); and practice (shared goals and learning as doing).

We know that mindfulness works. But not all companies are taking note. They should.

Mindful leadership enables managers to be mindful to ourselves, employees, customers, and the changing market needs and, from this place, to create workplaces that engage talented people and enable them to express themselves, to be creative, and to form innovative products and services of added value to customers and the market.

Like these corporate examples of the new world of mindfulness at work, we need a post-heroic leadership form that puts the emphasis on equal, more-shared, mutual, and less-hierarchical relationships between leaders and their teams.

In contrast to traditional models, which emphasize the influence of the leader's position on others, the contextual interaction of a truly mindful leadership form is expressed through flexible and variable collaboration rather than contribution. This view holds that leadership can exist in different directions and forms, blurs the distinction between leader and team member, and therefore offers a mutually-reflexive process. This notion also recognizes that nonhierarchical relationships such as a peer group or a social network that supports and nurtures can have influence just as a leader can.

In light of this changing dynamic, new and mindful leadership is required.

3

FROM EXTERNAL POWER TO INTERNAL STRENGTH

Mindfulness is all about getting personal.

The scientific benefits of mindfulness are well studied, and these benefits all come back to personal growth rather than strategic action. Becoming mindful creates the foundation for the kinds of positive personal habits that matter in the workforce rather than the superficial skills that can be learned and memorized.

What do I mean by this? Well, let's look at some proven empirical results.

Increased focus. In one study, researchers examined how mindfulness meditation affected people's ability to focus and not be distracted. The study compared a group that practiced meditation with a control group and found that the mindful participants performed significantly better across different focus variables. Mindful meditation increases the quality of attention and memory and decreases repetitive thoughts.[1]

Awareness. After a ten-day meditation workshop, participants in another study reported higher awareness and fewer depressive symptoms or bad moods, and they were less affected by mind wandering.[2]

Stress reduction. Many studies show that mindfulness reduces stress and anxiety. In one, researchers made participants watch a sad movie. Participants who had taken a mindfulness course had much lower levels of anxiety and depression while watching the movie compared with those who had not.[3]

Emotional regulation. Studies support the idea that regular meditation reduces emotional reactivity. In a study using functional MRI (fMRI) tests, it was found that a group that practiced meditation had a less active emotional response to startling films compared to others. These findings suggest that mindfulness meditation alters people's ability to use emotional regulation strategies in a way that allows them to experience emotions selectively.[4]

Better relationships. Research shows that a mindful person may experience a higher level of satisfaction in a relationship because of his or her ability to communicate and respond well to pressures created in the relationship. This suggests that mindfulness protects against the stress that can arise from conflicts in relationships.[5]

All these life skills, if we think about them carefully, are critical to the modern workplace. And what we know from the Tantalus story in chapter 1 is that if any of this is going to work, people need freedom in order to self-organize and think for themselves, as well as to get in touch with how their emotions are affecting their actions. Instead of settling on individual relationships in the corporate hierarchy, people need to be able to act like independent agents who can move freely, shop around for tasks, and take responsibility for what matters to them.

INTERNAL STRENGTH AND STRONG CORPORATE CULTURES

The basic premise of creating internal strength is, in organizational terms, to aim for a better culture at work. In essence, mindfulness can help to create a holacracy instead of a bureaucracy. People are autonomous beings who manage themselves, and the concept of holacracy is based on the fact that self-management allows employees to work together in groups without a lot of oversight. High levels of autonomy have been found to correlate with great efficiency and high levels of personal motivation.

But to do this well, areas of responsibility and priorities must be clear, well defined, transparent, and well communicated. People want to feel that they have an impact, and they need power and freedom of action to make this work. In addition, authority needs to be informal and based on the leader's ability to make connections with, persuade, and motivate others to act in ways that may or may not be convenient for them, such as giving up limited resources or acting against their personal interests in the short term.

So how do we unpack this and make it work?

Empowerment means releasing employees' self-motivation and increasing their responsibility. It requires encouraging employees to think, experience, and improve so that they *feel* they have autonomy and choice, and so they actually *have* autonomy and choice.

This new form of power is increasingly based on shared management between the individual and the organization from a holistic perspective. Such co-management is based on the ability of people/employees to better manage themselves while interacting with the needs and wishes of the organization. In this way, employees and managers can be attentive to their emotions, feelings, and thoughts—their inner world—by using mindfulness, which will allow them to authentically create appropriate solutions for the organization: their outer world.

In the end, the *intention* from where the leader acts is more important than his or her *behavior*. If a leader's intention is to advance the agenda of the organization without really listening to employees and solely to control the employees and the bottom line, it just doesn't work. But if the leader's intention is based on seeing and connecting with each person and allowing authentic interaction, then change is possible.

Therefore, leadership is all about self-management. We must be able to manage our inner world, emotions, thoughts, and time resources. And the basis for our ability to manage ourselves lies in mindfulness, because it creates a mindset that is attentive to the here and now.

WHERE DID MINDFULNESS COME FROM?

Mindfulness is based on Buddhist teachings that emerged 2,500 years ago as a way to solve human suffering, but their application to modern life might be traced back to 1979 and the work of Jon Kabat-Zinn, an American professor of medicine. That year he founded the Mindfulness Center at the University of Massachusetts for the Medical Professions in order to use this ancient tradition to treat chronic disorders that could not be adequately addressed by allopathic care. With his team, Kabat-Zinn developed Mindfulness Based

Stress Reduction (MBSR), which included eight two-hour sessions of various meditations, and offered the program to hospitals for patients dealing with chronic pain, stress, and anxiety who felt without hope. MBSR showed promising clinical results in treating generalized anxiety disorder, panic, and chronic pain.

Today the use of MBSR has spread to hundreds of hospitals, including major US health care institutions such as Kaiser Permanente. It is used in a variety of contexts in addition to medicine, such as clinical psychology, law, military, education, and even sports.

There are seven general tenets to MBSR work, known as the attitudes. These attitudes are what we strive for when we undertake to become more aligned with mindfulness.

1. Non-judging is the process of moving away from relying on our opinions of ourselves and of others and instead feeling our emotions.
2. Patience is engaging with the experiences of life without a timeline in mind.
3. Using a so-called "beginner's mind" is looking at each experience without prejudice or previous ideas.
4. Trust is having an intrinsic understanding of your own authority and worth.
5. The concept of non-striving allows the individual to focus on the experience over the outcome.
6. Acceptance allows the individual to see issues as they stand rather than as something that must change.
7. The process of letting go is being able to sit back and let the experience happen as it will rather than as we will it to be.

Let's be clear, mindfulness and meditation do not always require emptying our minds of thoughts entirely. This kind of deep work is the purview of Buddhist meditators, monks who have been practicing it for decades.

What the practice of meditation does is allow us to create a space between our thoughts. It is about finding presence through a deep listening and openness beyond the thinking person's personal and historical perception. In the Sufi tradition—the mystical tradition of Islam—presence simply describes the process of opening the heart. As it is called in Greek, *agape*, it is the highest form of love, unconditional love, love that does not depend on external conditions. This allows the release of old identities and the formation of new knowledge. It can allow the field to change, and the forces that shape the situation can shift from a state of reproduction of the past to a situation where a future emerges, is formed, and consequently is fulfilled. It can decrease or eliminate the boundaries between the self and others.

This is real internal strength because it is based on being able to open the heart, to listen to our emotions and feelings that arise with regard to each situation we face openly, and sometimes to make really difficult choices.

Retreat help. From a Buddhist perspective, a retreat is an intense meditation period—day, days, weeks, or years—in a quiet, remote place. It is also a safe place. We can choose to consciously retire from any distracting external activity in order to focus inward.

But from a modern point of view, retreat means retiring from daily life, detaching and staying in a place that allows for pause, respite, and introspection. A retreat can include various body awareness techniques, such as Tai Chi, yoga, Feldenkrais, and others. A retreat can even be a walk away from the noise, a day-to-day break, whether through connecting with nature or simply retreating to a quiet place.

INTERNAL STRENGTH IS POWER

The power of mindfulness derives from the systematic cultivation of our attention.

And that's what we need right now in business.

We live in a world of distraction, and much has already been said about the chaotic reality in which we have to manage. We call it VUCA, an environment characterized by volatility, uncertainty, complexity, and ambiguity. It is an environment characterized by the accelerated development of technologies and artificial intelligence (AI), which is growing at a dizzying pace. Organizations are now having to compete in the boundless economy of time and space in worldwide markets that are constantly linked to information. The evolution of technology blurs the boundaries between countries, organizations, and people; the ability to move among jobs, organizations, and countries is becoming more accessible and simpler than it was in the past.

There is an abundance of offers and opportunities for everyone, and there are new generations entering the working world and thus changing the rules.

Through mindfulness, we can recognize at any moment how we react. Mindfulness allows us to see our implicit and automatic patterns of thinking and behavior, as well as the results they create. By identifying these patterns, we can decide to change course.

Mindfulness contributes to adaptability, flexibility, and a capability to think and perceive clearly and quickly in changing situations.

But to be effective in using mindfulness and finding true strength rather than a false sense of power over others, leaders must consciously extract themselves from automatic behavior and respond to changing realities in more sophisticated ways. Leaders need to learn to cultivate and change themselves. This personal development amounts to enhancement of our inner capabilities as a broader intellectual understanding and perceptual ability, as well as a great ability to innovate, manage, and direct ourselves.

Internal strength is power because it opens us up to knowledge and wisdom resulting from interaction and relationships. In real life, there is no single leadership truth but instead a multitude of realities with which we must contend every day. Every stakeholder has their own perspective, and values can clash. In our present reality, when we wish to solve adaptive and complex problems, the solutions are often created by interactions among different people. Some call this organizational wisdom, a collective and interactive process. Internal strength is power because it suggests that an organization can be a place of integration, collaboration, and understanding of relationships; a sense of relativity and uncertainty; the ability to learn from one another's experience, sensitivity, and needs.

"Mindfulness is about being awake in our lives," says Kabat-Zinn. "It is about perceiving the exquisite vividness of each moment."

So, how do we build this internal strength, and the strength we need to navigate the quickly changing working world in which we operate? In the next chapter we'll explore exactly what we're looking for—and how to get started.

4

THE FOUNDATION OF
MINDFUL LEADERSHIP

G reen Market was founded by David Yeung in Hong Kong in 2001. That year, veganism became his focus. Letting go of eating meat occupied Yeung's thoughts as he discovered the connection between his own existence, changes in weather patterns, and what he knew about the food industry. He would arrive at restaurants where no vegan food was served, which made him uncomfortable.

"Whenever I went to eat with my family, friends, or people from work, they would treat veganism as problematic, Yeung told me. "Being vegan and not eating meat is very difficult for many people. Especially in Asian cultures, the word 'vegan' is a word that has a negative connotation. Vegan eating is seen as old-fashioned, boring, and unattractive."

By 2012, with cofounder Francis Ngai, David had launched Green Monday, an innovative global social venture that took on climate change, food insecurity, health issues, and animal welfare with a diverse platform that shifts individuals, communities, and corporations toward sustainable, healthful, and mindful living. Green Monday's goal was to change the entire dining system and create a new image of healthful, sustainable food by simply choosing to eat vegan once a week. A few years later he introduced Green Common—the world's first plant-based green living destination—to introduce a revolutionary food and lifestyle experience. The Green Monday movement has now spread to more than thirty countries, with three million people practicing Green Monday at its Hong Kong origin.

Yeung had realized that sustainability was not just a donation, and that innovation was needed to empower people and help them exchange old habits for new ones. "You can't tell people not to drive, not to use electricity, and settle for it," he says. "You have to offer them an alternative, what they can do differently to change their habits and behavior."

The movement now spans more than thirty countries from Thailand, Singapore, and China to Canada and the United States. Yeung's team helps raise awareness of veganism with companies such as Google and Adobe and schools and universities like UC Berkeley. They've developed plant-based "pork" to fuel Chinese demand. "It was important for us to see how to substitute pork instead of telling people to stop eating pork—because here pork is ubiquitous," Yeung explained. "What we do is offer an alternative by empowering people to replace regular pork with plant-based technology and innovation-based pork. The taste is the same but without the meat itself."

Everything Yeung does is driven by a vision of a better future. "Everything goes in the direction of people, planet and profit," he says. "The thinking that underpins our practice is how we disseminate knowledge, help people change consumption habits and increase environmental awareness—not just speeches, but practical solutions and tools for companies and people to be green. Not only is it inspiring, but it is also important to empower them and be innovative and turn reality around."

WHAT MINDFUL LEADERSHIP MEANS IN REAL TERMS

There are three distinctive characteristics of mindful leadership that we're aiming to build toward, and that Yeung's story illustrates.

Being present. Mindfulness is the ability to be present in this moment and be fully aware. Presence is a mental state in which we are connected to a narrow vision, experience, emotion, or process; at the same time, we are connected to a broad viewpoint beyond the self—the big picture.

Holding tension. This means we must be comfortable without knowing all the right answers, and without knowing the outcomes before we start a project. The challenge is developing an ability to live with imperfection, to allow movement and flow to take place rather than to seek certainty.

Being a servant. Servant leadership isn't new,[1] but it is intrinsically connected to mindfulness. Leadership needs to be a process aligned with the voluntary act of serving others, and responsibility in servant ethics means allowing every part of the company's actions to become overt and transparent. Servant leadership, which we'll talk more about in the next chapter, is about individuals working together, recognizing the value of each role.

To be successful, entrepreneurship requires us to embrace being in a state of unknown, mindful or not. Yeung succeeded because he focused on innovation, but also because he was passionate about his ideas. Even so, he credits mindfulness with affording him the presence of mind to take advantage of opportunities and to shift toward a holistic approach to business in which he was able to shift his attention to what mattered to build toward the future he wanted to see in the world.

Yeung's story boils down to the fact that he attaches importance to the ability to be fully engaged in life, and that attachment embodies all the characteristics of mindful leadership.

Anyone can be a leader. A person can be leader of a process, a product, a team, an idea he or she wants to promote. There is no longer a single leader who drives the ship. But connected to this new way of thinking, it can be argued that leadership is created at the moment in the context in which it is being held. Although the ship is driven by the CEO, leadership of the organization's members—on all levels—is also necessary.

But to be a leader of any kind, first we must manage ourselves.

The foundation of leadership is to manage our inner world, which includes our thoughts, feelings, emotions, and attention management. We have to do it every moment. This is true whether we understand mindfulness or not.

At the heart of self management, mindfulness of self and to others makes the process easier. It helps us develop the ability to be aware of the experience as it occurs and to become aware of it in a nonjudgmental way.

In the end, we want to make sure that we can manage our experiences—and ensure that our experiences do not manage us.

LEADERSHIP STARTS FROM THE INSIDE OUT

I teach fifteen types of meditation within my Mindfulness Based Leadership course, which consists of theory, reflection, and practice.

"Fifteen?" you might say, incredulously. And you might be right. But after teaching the course at organizations like Siemens, Check Point Software Technologies, Verint Systems, Neopharm, and others, I have come to realize that moving toward mindful leadership means, first and foremost, committing to meditation. My aspiration for everyone is to connect to a specific type of meditation that fits them, because meditation is the core practice that strengthens our ability to be present during the moments of the day.

Let's look at a few of the primary types of meditation so that you can start to get comfortable with this idea, because it will come up a lot in this book as we move forward.

Focus meditation. In this kind of meditation, our focus is on one thing; that focus can be on the breath, the body, a mantra, or an image. Our aim is to see our own thoughts, to give them some space, and to release them with breath. An appropriate metaphor for this is being on a high mountain. When we are on a high mountain, there are clouds. When a cloud arrives, we see it coming, we immerse in the cloud, and then it passes. We don't grasp the cloud and hold it. The metaphor of the cloud is an image of thought that you can let pass. The idea is not to start delving into thought but to just acknowledge it and release it.

Open awareness meditation. This approach is about the ability to be present in everything there is—sounds and mirrors, thoughts and feelings, without trying to eliminate them. We must accept them as they are and know they will pass. The idea of this meditation is to acknowledge everything that is happening right now without judging whether it is good or bad. For example, the noise of an air conditioner, the chirping of birds, the blowing wind, or whatever happens. In this kind of meditation, there are many more anchors where you can focus your attention at this moment.

Body scan meditation. This is a guided meditation in which you move your attention along the body, focus on a different part of the body, and look at it. There are feelings and emotions that arise around each part, and we look at them without judging them but simply allowing them to be as they are.

These are only a few of the meditative practices out there. There are other ways to experience meditation: It can happen while we are walking, eating, brushing out teeth, or washing the dishes. The idea is to be fully in the moment. For example, as you brush your teeth, you can feel the taste of the toothpaste, the water that enters your mouth, and the experience of brushing.

Ultimately, the purpose of every moment of our lives is to be in meditation; namely, to be fully present in the action we perform. The same is true in our personal and professional lives.

For example, if I face an angry coworker at my office, I may be able to draw on my awareness of my own emotions and practice non-judging and patience so that I don't react in anger on a behavioral level, thus decreasing the anger in the room and ensuring that my own stress levels do not go up as well. Similarly, if I find that I am upset with something a family member does, I may be able to trust my own inner worth and understand that their actions are likely not about me but about their own challenges. In this way, I may be able to be a resource to those around me rather than someone who escalates stress.

Mindfulness is therefore a practice that will be able to serve us over the long term in all situations.

DO YOU HAVE YOUR FOUNDATION IN PLACE?

To build our foundation, we must know how to manage ourselves and choose our desired responses to achieve the goals we set for ourselves rather than working from a place of automatic response. I call this part of ourselves the "automaton": a place of automatic reaction rather than of choice and engagement with ourselves. Our foundation needs to be a place of action rather than reaction, so we must move away from our automaton selves to our mindful selves.

Don't be confused. Our goal is not to bend reality. On the contrary, it is getting deeper into a reality in which we can listen to our emotions, experience, feelings, or thoughts and use them to navigate the world around us. As the space for mindfulness expands, we can set aside automatic behavior and choose the behavior we desire.

Getting to this state can put us in a position that is not easy, especially for managers who have been educated for years about how they are supposed to know the answer to where they want to take the organization. Today managers are required to know what the vision is and to what they aspire, but deep down we know that, for the most part, we do not really know how a vision will actualize.

In the next chapters we're going to go through the process of building toward mindful leadership step by step. We'll look at all the personal and organizational tools you can employ in order to become present, hold tension, and allow yourself to become a servant leader. At the end of each chapter, we'll review what you need to take away so that you can apply mindful leadership principles in your organization.

5

PARADOXICAL
MANAGEMENT

Only a life lived for others is worth living.

—Albert Einstein

About a decade ago, I decided to join a friend's retreat. It was a planned weekend for people to take time out. At that time in my life, I needed to get to know new people and expand my circle of friends, so I decided to go. I left without an agenda, aiming to just have fun.

The interesting thing was that the retreat had a significant impact on my life. I learned how to meditate more fully and contemplate things outside of my day-to-day life experience. I spent time by myself at many points over the weekend. I deliberated on the meaning of what I was doing as a business leader. I created the space for new ways of building relationships, and I found that I was drawn to different people than in the past.

Maybe because I went there with no specific goals, a space was formed for connections that I did not expect. I ended up with not only a new set of life tools but also a handful of business cards and a set of new contacts for when I reentered the "real" world.

This is the opposite of what most people do when they want to forge new business links.

For example, think about the average CEO aiming to expand the business and open branches overseas. She has a strategy of exactly how to do it and whom to make contact with. She is determined to land a list of customers or strategic partners through uninterrupted courtship and perseverance. She'll go to a conference with that list in hand, tracking down each lead one by one. But being so goal-oriented blinds her to the many other opportunities and possibilities all around her. The conference is filled with people she may not know, but who represent better business opportunities with a more organic fit with her own company. And yet her tight schedule means she's unaware of what she is missing.

The new skill of mindful leadership includes the ability to assess these situations in parallel. Using courage to stop responding to opportunities in an automatic way, to start listening to our inner feelings and confusion, is not an obvious choice. This is because doing so requires us to give up control, to be uncertain, and even to be able to let go.

Let me tell you what this feels like.

In the past I partnered with someone I thought would be my business partner. We had a big vision of working together. However, as the days passed by, it became clear that we were not a good fit. We thought too differently and saw the business world from different points of view. Although diversity of thought could be a good thing, there was too much of a gap between us. In my mind, I fully understood that we were not a good fit. However, emotionally it was very difficult to let go of the vision I had in mind; it was clear that I wanted to hold on to the story I was telling myself at the beginning of our relationship.

Although it's worthwhile to get past that barrier, it's the most challenging thing to accomplish in real life, at least for me. We have to develop the ability to know where we are heading, without knowing exactly how we will get there. It requires us to be open-minded and willing to experience uncertainty throughout the process, all the way until the moment things start to clarify.

Letting go and accepting what is, instead of what you wish, is an emotionally challenging process. This is the ability to accept that things don't always go the way we want them to go.

And it is an ongoing process.

In my courses I ask my students to relive this kind of experience—namely, the clinging part of us—and also the need to let go. At first I ask participants to think about a situation in which they have succeeded and were pleased with themselves and invite them to let go of the thought and instead feel it in their body, in their sensations, and in their emotions. I then ask them to bring to mind an experience in which they haven't succeeded, in which in their perception they have failed. Then I invite them to let go of the thought and process it in their body, in their sensations, and in their emotions again.

When I do this exercise myself, I actually feel it in my body; usually these memories arise with feelings of frustration, anger, disappointment, and more. I am happy when these feelings all go away, or when the time for the exercise is over. However, when practicing the positive experience, my body is alive with great energy that I don't want to end. In either case, the act of acknowledging this feeling of not wanting to let go, of clinging and the desire for this feeling to stay, is part of understanding everything we experience through embodiment. Our inclination is to hold on to things that feel good or sometimes things that feel bad, depending on what matters to us at the time.

Life is continually changing, though. It's the understanding that all things are impermanent—our negative experiences as well as the positive ones—that matters. It's like the saying that you can't get in the same river twice because the river is continuously changing. As we let go, we can experience life fully.

DOING THROUGH BEING

The working world is filled with contradictory emotions: conflicts, anxiety, frustration, boredom, and insignificance along with joy, commitment, and interest.

But focusing only on the positive side of the human experience in organizations not only flattens the great diversity and richness of work life but ignores the paradoxical nature, and the value, of a diverse work experience. This experience may include negative feelings along with positive ones, and that's okay. A commitment to paradoxical moments gives us a sense of meaning and connection that provides us with various possibilities for action.

In this context, the ability of a leader to support dialectical tension, to succeed in an experience of uncertainty, and to allow a solution to emerge from listening to different voices leads to the formation of new knowledge.

Today's corporate world is characterized by many paradoxes and tensions we have to confront, such as short-term versus long-term tension, gaps between speed and quality, or gaps between risk-taking and security. Each of these contradictory elements is logical on its own, but when they come together, an irrational absurdity is created. The ability to enable paradoxes to exist allows for innovation, variability, and dynamism, as well as personal and organizational growth, to prevail.

The contribution of paradoxical thinking to managerial thinking, therefore, is its ability to inspire creativity and encourage change. This encourages a shift from modern management, based on planning and control, to postmodern management, which emphasizes the creation of meaning within a complex reality.

Presence and mindfulness are characterized, in part, by paradox as well.

As managers, we have always learned that we need to do the right things, to promote and push people, projects, and processes. This means we may become too focused on doing. Mindful leadership, however, is characterized by an inward awareness of the self and an outward awareness of a need for supporting the development of others. In essence, a mindful leader has to confront the tension between doing and being. This means being able to be present while listening, but also taking a step further into actualizing this presence in realistic business terms.

Mindful leadership is paradoxically driven rather than goal-driven. It respects a leader's need to be strong in the sense of a firm knowledge of direction, but pairs this with a clear conception of the leader's own values, the company's values, and the ability to let go.

This approach can be linked back to the subtle and profound notion of *wu wei*, or non-doing, in Taoist philosophy. This concept describes a situation where a person uses the least energy possible to cope with the stressors of life. This does not mean an individual has to refrain from any actions but rather must abstain from acting against the natural courses of the external world. The purpose is to generate a balance between one's inner and outer worlds. *Wu wei* requires spontaneity and noninterference as things flow in their natural course.

These are all important qualities for effective performance. Maintaining balance is a key to effectiveness.

PARADOXICAL LEADERSHIP: BECOMING THE SERVANT

Robert Greenleaf, whose early essays were assembled to create the seminal servant leadership text, *The Power of Servant Leadership*, believed that leadership is a process most accurately demonstrated by those who are engaged in the voluntary act of serving others. According to Greenleaf, leadership is not delegated, it is assumed: "If there are sanctions to compel or induce compliance, the process would not qualify as leadership. The only test of leadership is that somebody follows—voluntarily."[1] Leadership roles and positions are thus fluid and informed by the circumstances and interpersonal relations and experiences that constitute project implementation.

Companies are often led by individuals who are driven by such a need for financial success that they manipulate the company's operations and the people around them. According to Greenleaf, responsibility in servant ethics would necessitate drawing aside the veil of context and construct and allowing every part of the company's actions to be transparent. Service thus becomes closely affiliated with working together in contrast to the polarizing positions of worker and manager, hence the paradox.

To this end, the concept of mindful leadership argues that a leader should be committed to the development of others because she or he understands that the success of the organization rests on the capabilities and commitment of employees. Such leadership is a force that evokes feelings of attraction, magic, pleasure, and concern for the work and the people in the work environment, driven by inspiration expressed through commitment to the organization and its productivity. In being mindful, a leader must present financial results that allow the organization to exist but, at the same time, work for a broader set of interests: social justice, environmental sustainability, positive development of humanity, and peace.

Servant leadership is not a concept that should be confined to a mere few conscious-driven people. In fact, we're seeing more companies acknowledge this.

In August 2019 the Business Roundtable, a coalition of the CEOs of the largest US companies, issued the following statement headed by JPMorgan's Jamie Dimon: "From today on, the main goal of a corporation is not to promote the interests of shareholders. Now companies need to invest in employees as well, to create value for consumers and work with suppliers fairly and ethically."[2] The statement is signed by two hundred CEOs, including those of Apple, American Airlines, Bank of America, Boeing, and AT&T.

When people are driven by the desire to provide service, they do so as a selfless act of love that mindfulness practitioners call "self-transcendence."

Self-transcendence is the process of expanding one's boundaries beyond a selfish point of view, toward an open consciousness that creates a deepening sense of unity and partnership. When we transcend ourselves, we serve employees, colleagues, and customers. Being a servant for the greater good creates a situation in which we become part of something beyond ourselves—something truly meaningful.

Simon Sinek, the American-British author of *Start with Why*, suggests that meaningfulness is the "why" that underlies the work we do, or that should be at the heart of our efforts in the world. In a TED lecture he gave, he talked about the fact that most organizations and leaders are busy selling their product or service from the wrong direction. Company leaders are too focused on what they are selling rather than on why they exist and whom they serve.

Service leadership, therefore, represents the intention of the mindful leader. While some managers do everything by prescription, this makes their work mechanical, without the deep intent of achieving something that matters. The more one acts out of greater connection to oneself and one's motivations, the more one can become connected to a place of service and pure intention.

There are still organizations that use social responsibility as a form of public relations—for example, to demonstrate that they operate from a place of service and giving—but the intention from which they operate is unclear, sometimes even manipulative. These are old paradigms, and they fail to look toward the future. A mindful leader, instead, is driven by service for the purpose of business and not only by motives of power or money. Leaders of this nature focus on "we" rather than "me." They are leaders through mentoring, human development, and inspiration, bringing transformation into the organization and making the best of those around them. They understand that their job is to serve the best purpose of the organization, to support people in the organization, and to create value for all interested parties.

STEP ONE: ACCEPT PARADOXICAL LEADERSHIP

Mindful leaders strive to produce the maximum benefit to all interested parties at the same time, but they know that one interested party is not a victim of another. They operate according to Triple Bottom Line principles—profit, people, and planet—or similar thoughtful frameworks. These organizations work with the environment and people in mind, and often strive for a profit-to-employee ratio so that employees' personal goals are aligned with the organization's financial goals.

As leaders and individuals, ask yourself the following:

- What is important for me? What is my "why"? My purpose?
- What is the added value, as a company, we are offering to our business and social communities?
- How can I better serve my employees, customers, and community?
- Do I act according to my stated values and belief systems?
- If the answer is no, what can I do differently in order to close the gap?
- When I set goals, what are the ways in which I achieve them? Am I open to various ways to achieve these goals, or am I focused only on the way I already know?
- When I set a meeting, do I listen to the various voices of my employees or mainly speak to my own agenda?
- When in conversation, how much of the time am I listening and asking questions and how much do I speak? If the answer is "I am speaking most of the time," try practicing active listening and asking questions at least 50 percent of the time.
- Lastly, do I dare to not know the answers to these questions?

6

FLEXIBLE MINDSET

Those who flow as life flows know they need no other force.

—Lao Tzu

With the natural selection of our species, we experience preserved, automatic life patterns and mechanisms that allow us to survive.

But many of these patterns no longer fit or are helpful to us. A good example is our craving for refined sugar. In our collective past, we craved sugar, mainly from fruit on trees, because it was essential to our survival and provided us with energy. But today the context of our lives has changed and we have access to an excess of sugar-filled empty carbohydrates. Our automatic behaviors do not necessarily fit, and we quickly become overweight when we follow those cravings.

Similar patterns are evident in business. For example, a manager who is supposed to compile a report at the end of each month might think she doesn't need to think about how to fill out that report every time, as it does not require much energy and time investment. But what if that report was about employee performance or a product launch? It might serve the company and employees better if she gave the report thought, time, and critical attention. These behaviors might also include automatically saying no to every new opportunity, working solely to please others, giving up our voices to avoid clashes, exploding in the face of any disagreement or confrontation, and so forth.

Automatic behavior can be a simple act that we do without distraction, without thinking twice. But it is also part of our agenda, because this behavior saves us time and means we don't have to try so hard. But automatic actions do not serve us when we want to produce new results and try new ways forward.

Automatic habits can lead to stagnation.

Instead, we must stop and examine what is happening to be consciously able to manage and bring about innovative and creative results.

Here's an example from my personal life. I'm someone who finds herself automatically saying no to every new opportunity. About five years ago a colleague started a mindfulness course at Tel Aviv University. Another colleague suggested that I should attend the course and collect examples for a book I had planned to write. I immediately told myself no; I have nothing to learn there at all. My automaton immediately wanted to push away from the opportunity, claiming that I already knew everything about the subject. Even so, I pushed myself to attend the course and assisted my colleague in collecting and writing the material. I just went to be there, to learn and help. During the course's last session, I met a visiting professor in Hong Kong who had developed a Master's program in leadership that included a thirty-hour mindfulness course; he invited me to teach there. This opportunity opened a whole new window in my career and a new world of work.

We live in a dynamic era that requires us to be able to manage flexibly and embrace continuous learning and development, and mindfulness can help us create a flexible mindset and help us release automatic patterns more easily.

Focused mindfulness is "a specific nonjudgmental awareness of present-moment stimuli without cognitive elaboration"[1] that has been used in alignment with meditation and has been a major part of traditional psychotherapy from the time of Freud. The practice of meditation helps people find awareness in the everyday experiences of consciousness itself, including all the senses.

In fact, studies of electrical brain activity before and after an eight-week mindfulness meditation program indicate that meditation can cause changes in both brain function and immune levels in the body. According to these studies, the type of mindfulness program is not relevant. The same results have been found within the brain activity of both Buddhist meditators and Christian nuns.[2]

A number of experimental studies in the United States have indicated that the daily practice of mindfulness may also help improve memory and cognition, mood, and overall mental health. For example, a study at Wake Forest University School of Medicine found that even brief mindfulness training over a span of four days can significantly improve visuospatial processing, working memory, and executive functioning.[3] Other research has shown that individuals who took part in a mindfulness training component built skills like self-care, attention to well-being, self-awareness, cognitive behavior therapy skills acquisition, and empathy and compassion.[4]

All these benefits allow human beings to become flexible in their mindset and garner the ability to make better choices in a modern life.

FLEXIBILITY AND REFLECTION HAVE TO START FROM THE START

For people to be flexible, they have to be reflective.

We often see reflection—time given to ourselves to just stop for a second and write down or explore our thoughts creatively—as a waste of time. But that's wrong.

Reflection results in more money and fewer costs, more innovation and more breakthrough ideas that are truly disruptive, not just cannibalizations of existing product and service lines. The human experience should be honored in business. We need to give our people, our teams, a range of opportunities to listen to one another's stories. Companies need to build this into onboarding as well as into everyday meetings. It doesn't have to take a lot of time, either. During their Agile sprints every morning, members of one tech team tell each other about the best thing that happened to them in the past twenty-four hours: a child coming home with their best grade, a great piece of cake, a marriage proposal, a cold-morning 10k run over the weekend.

The goal is to have all the information we need for effective shifts, but recognizing that that information isn't necessarily at the end of a spreadsheet. We know that people need to feel connected to really get curious; they need to feel that it is okay, and right, and normal to share their most deviating thoughts and ideas. We need to tell ourselves that this is okay.

A reflection practice is something that works to reduce friction, build up the capacity to decide with better information, and be present with the challenges we face.[5]

Curiosity has to start with the self. Neurological research shows that active self-reflection—where people take the time to consciously and continuously reflect on themselves and the needs of the company in any given situation—facilitates their ability to relate new information to prior knowledge and seek out new ideas. In empirical research using business case simulations and a reflection training intervention, a high level of self-reflection has been shown to correlate with direct performance on the job, as well as more consistently high outcomes in planning and decision making.[6] The same findings suggest that reflecting on what's possible, and building a reflective practice, allows people to make better decisions even when market conditions are exceptionally challenging. It also directly lowers costs. Reflection helps us decide what matters most so that we're apt to learn from our experiences.[7]

Research also shows that mindful decision makers are more open to feedback and less prone to misinterpret it by making self-serving choices, meaning that team engagement and community building can be leveraged to their full potential.[8]

Over time, if practiced daily, this approach has personal development effects that will prepare us for the future of work. Field research demonstrates just how powerful reflection is for what we expect for the future workplace, helping employees internalize broader multifaceted skills, including creativity, imagination, and entrepreneurship, achieving the most success in what is currently a highly competitive and congested global market.[9]

DYNAMIC AGILITY

The reality we face in the current business world requires organizations to be able to respond at a faster rate, perhaps one that allows for constant changes to be incorporated into what we create, sell, and do as teams.

Organizations must be agile.

"Agility," a term that is usually aligned with the high-tech industry, is the ability to move quickly and easily. An agile organization is one that can flexibly adapt itself to its market and environmental conditions by upholding high quality standards and outputs to the satisfaction of both the customer and the organization.

For the high-tech industry, a five-stage "Waterfall" model was usually employed in the past, one that outlines project requirements, design, implementation, verification, and maintenance and is characterized mainly by a serial process where each stage begins after the previous stage is completed. In this process, if a change is needed later in the process, the price of the change becomes higher.

The agile method, on the other hand, is seen as less structured and more flexible in terms of time. It emphasizes the work of short intervals ranging from one week to one month. From time to time, developers pause to get feedback and verify that they are working in the right direction. In this way, it is possible to change and correct throughout the development process and not just do it at the end. Agility works in rapid iterations characterized by the ability to move quickly, simply, and lightly.

And so it requires a changing, flexible mindset. We need to change quickly, not fall in love with our ideas. We have to know how to stop, examine things, and change.

A start-up company I worked with, let's call it Enigma, had two partners. They developed a product, raised money, and offered the product to customers. Over time, the partners realized that the product they developed was not sufficiently attractive and that they were operating in a bit of a red ocean: Their market was saturated. In this situation, a company must look for its added value and uniqueness over its competitors, requiring attention to customer needs. In Enigma's case, the partner responsible for sales encountered objections from those customers. He could have kept on pushing forward, but he chose to be mindful, facing the reality of customers' reactions. During this pause, he and his partner examined the market, listened to their customers, and decided on a pivot. They agreed to connect with a broader picture beyond their emotional attachment to their initial market approach, and despite sunk costs. (A sunk cost, in economics and business decision making, is a cost that has already been incurred and cannot be recovered. Individuals commit to the sunk cost fallacy when they continue a behavior or endeavor as a result of previously invested resources—time, money or effort. In other words, a sunk cost is a sum paid in the past that is no longer relevant to decisions about the future.)

Organizations of any type, not just those connected to technology, must be flexible and respond quickly to their customers' requirements. This means there should be a high level of harmony and collaboration between team members or between team members and the organization. Agile work addresses the need to be flexible and fast.

In order to lead in this dynamic reality, managers must be thoughtfully flexible and adopt a pattern of what is known as a "growth mindset." This term comes from research completed by Carol Dweck for her book *Mindset*.[10] She wrote that there are two mental states, fixed mindset and growth mindset, which help to define our personalities. A fixed mindset assumes that our character, intelligence, and creativity are as unchangeable as the qualities engraved on a rock. On that basis, success is seen as the endorsement of inherent intelligence. People with such awareness strive to succeed and avoid trying new things due to fear of failure. A growth mindset, on the other hand, is based on the assumption that your basic qualities can be nurtured through effort and determination. This view sees challenges as the basis for development and growth and not as a sign of intelligence. A growth mindset allows intelligence and personality to evolve. People with this perception see themselves as learning and developing.

A growth mindset sees everything we do as another experience that allows growth and development as a leader.

But think about a company for a moment. A company is designed fundamentally to fulfill a mission or goal. Because that goal usually has something to do with making money, I would argue that a company requires characters, rather than people, to take part in that fulfillment process. What I mean by this is that we're all supposed to take on a role—a character if you will—rather than be our authentic selves. That's because a company defines its values and the outcomes it wants to achieve in each year of its strategic plan so that it is easier to match people with roles in the organization. We slip into character assignments so that we can get hired for those roles, creating our own personal brands on LinkedIn or Twitter in order to perfectly fit the keywords recruiters are targeting. Social economists call this a company's embeddedness: The social context that governs everything a company does has definitions, keywords, character expectations, and rote experiences. Organizations have these defining characteristics, and as a result people are bound by these specific social roles. Unfortunately, once we slip into these characters, we are limited not only in our ability to shift in the best interest of our organization but also in our ability to see ourselves outside of our character role.

We need to break out of structure, of norms, of rules, and we need to be able to move as fast as the world around us does.

We must build a practice around opening the door to the kind of everyday decisions that can change our ability to adapt and let go of the fear of change. On this path we can shape the workplace of the future, one that is inevitably changing every moment—a future, even one five years from now, we can't even imagine or fathom, if we believe what those who are tracking human progress, change, and challenge tell us. These decisions don't have to be large, mind-bending ones in order to help us move toward success. I'm advocating for a different way of thinking about planning and strategizing for our lives and work practices, one that doesn't require revolution but rather an evolution: of intention, of reflection, and of conscious awareness of how we're moving forward.

In his book *Hit Refresh*,[11] Microsoft CEO Satya Nadella talks about how, at a large conference, a woman asked him why women's wages were less than those of men. In his reply, he quoted one of his teachers as saying that sometimes it is better to do the job; the remuneration will come later. After the conference, he was uncomfortable with the answer he had given. He recognized the opportunity he had missed to influence gender equality. Afterward, he sent an email to all Microsoft employees, writing that he realized he had missed the opportunity to positively influence the issue of pay equality between women and men, and sought to correct what he had said. His growth mindset revealed his capability in terms of self-reflection, contemplation, learning, and sharing his own insights.

It will be very difficult for managers and employees who do not adopt a growth mindset to survive in the contemporary corporate world, as well as to succeed and remain relevant. Because the reality we face, especially as we move through a global pandemic and social upheaval, is very dynamic and requires us to keep learning and moving out of our comfort zones. We need to adopt a mindset that will help us respond to the changing needs of customers, employees, and the market and be able to change and be changed. As leaders, we are required to move the team, the department, or the company forward and to harness employee interest and commitment.

STEP TWO: BUILD AN AGILE, FLEXIBLE MINDSET

In business, we should constantly strive to learn new things and not let the situation remain as it is. We need to change quickly. We need to *not* fall in love with our ideas. We need to know how to stop, examine things, and change when necessary. Being able to be present, listening to what is happening here and now, discovering mental flexibility, accepting new information without judgment—all of this enables innovative and creative ideas to emerge.

How can you start doing this?

Reflect on your life: It can be your personal life, work, relationships, or any other aspect of your life. See if you are satisfied with the different aspects of your life.

For instance, if you aren't satisfied with a relationship, reflect on it. Ask yourself what you don't like in this relationship and how you can change it. What can you do differently that will change the interaction? It doesn't need to be something big. It can be a small change, like saying no more often, being vulnerable, asking for help when you need it, or any other change that comes to mind.

Bring to mind a pattern of behavior, thought, or action that has served its purpose and is now limiting your future. Reflect about the habit and ways you can cope and change it.

Dare to get out of your comfort zone—learn a new skill, do something you've never done before. Challenge yourself.

Practice journaling. Take three pieces of paper, sit down, and write intuitively what's on your mind, without stopping. If you don't know what to write, simply write, "I don't know what to write." This kind of free writing enables us to clear our minds and make space for new insights to emerge and creativity to flow. If you have time, do it every day for ten minutes or so.

Create a routine in which every month or so, depending on your schedule, you meet with a new person. Meeting new people and being exposed to new themes and stories enable us to stay curious and open-minded and open the realms of opportunities.

As leaders, do the following:

- Ask for feedback from your employees regarding what works and what doesn't work.
- Be open to feedback and see it as an opportunity to learn and thrive.
- Create reflecting meetings; invite people to talk about conflicting issues or projects, not in a judgmental way but from curiosity and an open mind.
- Create stand-up meetings, a quick gathering in which everyone shares what he or she is working on right now. This practice connects the team to the broader picture and enables change and adaption as new processes emerge.
- Create a workplace environment that nourishes continuous learning. Offer your employees training and development programs to acquire new skills and sharpen their approach to work.

7

AUTHENTIC COMMUNICATION

At Tantalus, the management team had a strong desire to promote the issue of open and transparent communication. Even so, existing patterns suggested that the gap between wanting clear communication and actually achieving it was huge.

The company embarked upon creating different dialogue spaces and situations in which to start practicing this value. An employee in one of the meetings claimed that half the organization included people who actively tried not to express an opinion on anything unless the situation was dire and it was almost too late to address things.

This reflection characterizes the attitude of many employees at many companies in many places. People don't often tell the truth out loud, being afraid of what their boss will think of them. Even when they identify the issue and deal with it, there are barriers. Many organizations prefer to avoid such situations and continue business as usual.

As part of the discussion at Tantalus, the human resources manager stated that she hoped that open doors were the norm, from the CEO to the managers. She asked participants to look for solutions to encourage open communication. A 360-degree feedback program was suggested in which employees would receive feedback from coworkers, their direct supervisor, and subordinates, as well as suppliers, customers, and other stakeholders. But other participants thought there were too many barriers to even try. One manager, Gilad, suggested that his door was open and said, "I feel that if a situation is problematic, employees will contact me. I feel they will come if they are in crisis; and, yes, it is worth checking before we reach a point of no return."

The terms "explosion," "crisis," and "point of no return" are key here.

Because of communication barriers, people were acting from a point of view of fight or flight, storing feelings, emotions, thoughts, and anger within them instead of expressing them. The team felt lost.

Emotion is often seen as an inhibitor to business, a barrier that overflows and can interfere with desired goals. But often the opposite is true: Once emotions are given a place, connection, movement, and progress can be made toward a company's desired goals. It is important, of course, to decide on when and where to have this kind of communication. Equally important is the "how."

But in order for us to come to our workplace and fully express ourselves, we must give place to two channels of communication: the logical, causal, and rational communication channel, but also the emotional channel—the feelings, the experiences, and the values that often seem to lack legitimacy in the corporate world. The assumption is that this kind of communication delays the achievement of goals, and that it will give employees permission to share an explosion of emotions—anger, frustration or pain, joy and passion—creating a tap that cannot be shut off.

COMMUNICATION STARTS WITH THE SELF

Communication is a key tool in driving innovative, creative, and agile organizations. But what many do not truly understand is that this agility is based on trust relationships between people. Producing a healthy, harmonious, and successful company is achieved through the ability to produce constructive and authentic communication.

In mindful communication, we learn how to listen and manage our emotions, feelings, and thoughts.

This kind of communication involves listening to the self and the various sensations and emotions that arise within us during conversations. It is communication born of genuine listening, from a position of openness and curiosity, and without defensiveness. This communication transcends fear, and it enables change and growth and the ability to connect to a broad vision and create the groundwork for creative solutions to emerge.

But trust-building is harder, and more important, than it seems on the surface.

Trusting ourselves seems like one of those life challenges that only an elite few can really accomplish. But that's simply not true, and it's important that we understand just how much trusting ourselves, and others, matters to the workplace.

Part of the problem has to do with those characters we create for work and for life that we discussed earlier. An actor puts on a persona in order to create an illusion, but she's not the only one. Personality theory demonstrates that we often claim different personae in order to get a job we think is better. But is that job better for us or better for the social image we feel we have to fulfill? Neuroscience tells us that the stress of trying to remain in character leads to altered decision making. This is not the best outcome for businesses, or for ourself.

Authentic human connection at work, however, holds people accountable in a way that a team does not; it allows us to step out of our characters and into ideas that are more valuable, more aligned with innovation. Trust and innovation are clearly linked—we have to be able to trust ourselves to try and implement something new, bold, and different from norms. Loyalty and trust in all directions are lost arts that should count in our modern world because of the way they empower us individually and together. This creates the desire, motivation, and willpower you cannot build through a hierarchal, tightly controlled system.

Most organizations hold many, many meetings. The result, however, is often a waste of time and a lack of productivity. This may be because organizations try to promote a particular topic; everyone is so busy trying to convince their colleagues that they are right that they stop listening. This kind of communication is characterized by a perception of win/loss, and it doesn't advance innovation in any way. This is because, as researcher David Bohn tells us, the rules in a discussion are something like a ping-pong game in which we hit a ball back and forth between us.[1] Winning means the team accepts your opinion; it doesn't mean the best idea gets supported.

True communication requires people to be truly listening and balanced.

In real life this looks like people being emotionally connected to experiences, thoughts, or feelings (attachment), and simultaneously being able to look at themselves from a distance (detachment). In a dialogue, there is a free flow of meaning between people as a stream flows between two banks of a river, and the group can reach a larger pool of shared meaning and solutions the individual cannot reach. In this process, people can reflect on their own thoughts and develop a kind of sensitivity that goes far beyond what we usually know as thinking. This behavior requires people to be in a mental state of listening.

Yes, some people are more rational than others. Both types are equally valuable. The idea is to see who is truly in front of you, from a place of presence and without an agenda, so that you can use the discourse and language style of that person. If there is a very rational person in front of me and I focus solely on emotional discourse, we probably cannot have a fruitful conversation. In contrast, my ability to be here and now, listening to the person standing in front of me, will enable me to have open and meaningful communication with that person. The opposite is also true; someone who is unable to communicate rationally because they are emotionally overwhelmed is someone who needs to be met where they are.

The reality is that some people speak about facts and data when their real challenge is an emotional one. It's not always as obvious as tears or yelling.

Researcher Albert Mehrabian conducted a series of famous experiments in which he showed how different our verbal and nonverbal messages really are.[2] Mehrabian made observations in open spaces such as playgrounds and public spaces and concluded that there are three parameters that bring communication together: body language, intonation, and content. He mapped the impact of each component on our whole experience of communication, showing that, at 55 percent, body language is the source of more than half of what we communicate and hear when we talk to others; intonation influences 38 percent of what we hear, while the content of what we say has the least impact on communication, only 7 percent. How we say things is not just sometimes but always more important than what we say.

In my work I've accompanied investment consultants in their meetings at one of the largest banks in the world. I would sit next to them and listen to their conversations with customers and then provide feedback on the conversation, communication, and their behavior with the customer. I remember sitting with one investment consultant who was many years older than I and discussing how the long waiting times at the bank were causing great frustration and dissatisfaction among customers. A customer who called in had to wait about ten minutes, and he started complaining as soon as it was his turn. The consultant began to explain rationally and logically that there was a long queue and that they were doing their best, but this explanation did not convince the client, who continued complaining. About five minutes went by in wasted discourse, which only extended the waiting time the company wanted to prevent in the first place. After the conversation, I suggested that the next time a frustrated customer called, the consultant could use emotional, empathetic discourse and tell the client that he understood their frustration and that he would also be frustrated if he had to wait a long time. The consultant looked at me and realized he had no choice. Amazingly, after expressing empathy with the next customer, the consultant did not need to add another word. The customer immediately moved on to talk about her personal finances.

People want to be seen. Once you see them by expressing alignment with their emotional state, they will move on. If they are *not* seen, however, they will continue to argue. They may even use a rational form of discourse. But then they'll experience stagnation, because they aren't really getting what they wanted out of the conversation.

You may think this use of empathy is manipulative, and that the consultant played the game he was told to play. Let me say two things here. First of all, sometimes in order to learn a new skill, we need to do it in an unnatural way, against our automatic responses. We may feel artificial. But there is a point at which this behavior becomes part of who we are and our abilities. This conduct enables us to grow and expand our skills around empathy. Secondly, people respond to our intention. If I say I understand you but don't really understand you, the chance of your responding positively to my words is unlikely. Most people actually respond to what transmits beyond words, and if the intention is manipulative and insincere, it won't work.

In order to listen deeply and enable new knowledge to emerge, we need to create a dialogue space. What does this mean?

1. Be present mentally, emotionally, and physically. Bring yourself fully. Share how you see things mentally, and share what you feel and

experience through dialogue, even if these are feelings of inconvenience, excitement, frustration, or anything else.

2. Dare to be vulnerable. Have the courage to bring your authentic viewpoint and feelings into the room, even if you aren't sure how people will react.

3. Open your mind and heart to new ideas and views; put your assumptions aside and listen with curiosity to other ideas. Try to understand their viewpoint fully, with a beginner's mind and heart. Be open to letting go of your assumptions and enabling new wisdom to emerge.

4. Respect others. Make space for more opinions, even if at first you feel the urge to contradict them. Pause and listen. Enable other opinions to be present, and enable different perspectives.

5. Maintain uncertainty without setting it aside. Create space within yourself and through the dialogue for uncertainty. Don't push for a solution. Give legitimacy to not knowing the answers. It's okay not to find a solution right away.

The essence of listening in the dialogue space requires us to be mindful and present in the moment. Without an open will, it is highly doubtful that something new can emerge. This is a place of full presence in which we can become connected to what is vivid in this moment. We do not have to cling to opinions and ideas and agendas, and new wisdom can arise from that moment. This conduct requires us to have the abilities of reflection, curious listening, generosity toward the other side, and an attitude of openness. This allows time and space for a solution to emerge from the interaction among different people and perspectives. It requires us to embrace evolving thinking and be able to constantly examine our basic assumptions. Moreover, it requires us to be able to let go.

COMMUNICATION CONTINUES WITH INCLUSION

Today many organizations talk about inclusion and diversity, but do they actually achieve this goal?

Back at Tantalus, there was fear and a sense of panic in the room because people thought that expressing their own feelings might get them fired. An extended management meeting was called in order to create dialogue around the topic of fear of communication. Michael, the CEO, invited participants to speak authentically, and there was a shift in how people responded. People dared to question power relations at the company. They reflected on how the Israeli company was seen in the eyes of their American counterparts and expressed their frustration.

As an observer, I could feel the stress and anxiety increasing in the room as the dialogue progressed and people talked about what should not be spoken. When one of the managers accidentally dropped a pen, everyone burst out laughing; it was that challenging.

In the end, however, I could see how each team member strove to narrow the gap between their ideal and their actual identities in conversation. Self-awareness, empathy, vulnerability, and an openness to learn from others began to shape the conversation. Self-awareness allows us to shift because it allows us to practice in a way that is fundamentally adaptable, cutting out the noise of everything else.

There is freedom in self-awareness.

Many times, we are so caught up in the reality and stories we tell ourselves that we are not really connected to the experience that is taking place right now. It is not always easy to be mindful to what is happening with our naturally complicated feelings of sadness, pain, frustration, disappointment, and more. But it is sometimes the aversion to those complicated emotions that ultimately produces greater suffering

This can be connected back to the Buddhist parable of the arrows.

The Buddha equates pain and suffering with two arrows that hurt a person. There is the original arrow caused by external pain, such as an earthquake, divorce, death, sickness, and so forth. The second arrow arises as we inflict inner pain and suffering on ourselves. The first arrow is inevitable. We can't control it. We usually start to think, "Why did this happen to me?" We start to feel sorry for ourselves, resulting in the additional arrow, which we stick into ourselves. Our entanglement with ourselves does not change reality; it only brings us more suffering. The second arrow refers to our unwillingness to accept the situation as it is.

In business we call people insecure; we say they have low confidence, low self-esteem; we tell them to seek out the right information before suggesting something new. We hold them accountable to a structure that judges them for every move they make that seems outside the norm. We know we're vulnerable, but we don't want to show it.

By creating spaces of dialogue where employees can express their unique voices, beliefs, perceptions, and thoughts, managers show their *willingness* to accept the situation as it is.

These spaces promote the inclusion of diversity and the wisdom of each individual to lend themselves to organizational wisdom. Dialogue spaces are a containment environment in which employees can express dissatisfaction and tensions, providing space for continuous learning and self- and organizational reflection. They also constitute communities of practice.

Participation in these communities is a complex process that combines action, talking, thinking, emotions, and belonging. In other words, communities of practice constitute the space for shared learning, allowing people to be present in the moment, and to bring themselves fully to the table. In this experience of interaction, participation is a source of identity. By identifying our mutual relationships, we become part of one another.

STEP THREE: CREATE SPACE FOR DIRECTIONLESS COMMUNICATION

Spaces for dialogue make it possible to express emotions at work. Employees can interact, express, listen, change, promote organizational change, connect to the broad picture, and develop through one another. This behavior enables the organization to contain these changes and achieve stable dynamism, which allows for new concepts to emerge and strive, to form and change at the edge of chaos. Most innovation occurs at the meeting point between order and chaos. It will not create anarchy, but will instead generate constant learning, development, and movement, enabling the organization to remain dynamic and respond to changing realities and demands.

Strive for direct communication with people. If you sense a challenging feeling with your employees, colleagues, or manager, approach them and dare to share these feelings. Communicate fully—emotionally and logically—when disagreeing with someone.

Try this three-step model as a means of reaching this place of clarity:

1. Reflect the other party's feelings back to them, and the rational explanation for this. For example: "Yossi, I understand that you are frustrated with the quality of the product because you expected that after the time we were working, the product wouldn't have any programming bugs."
2. Express your own feelings about the situation and the rational explanation for it. For example: "At the same time, I feel disappointed that when I approached you along the way asking for help, I didn't receive a response because you were busy."
3. Look for two or three possible alternatives. "I suggest that we consider what options we currently have for improving the product in the time available." Aim for a win-win solution.

As leaders, how can we encourage this kind of communication?

- Create transparent communication with your employees, even in challenging times when not everything is clear. Acknowledge what's known and what's not known. Transparent communication creates clarity for employees and contains uncomfortable feelings.
- Start meetings with a checkup. Ask each participant, on a scale of 1 to 10, "How present are you right now?"
- Dare to be present and vulnerable in the meeting and share what you are currently experiencing without knowing a solution in advance.
- Be respectful, open, and mindful to other opinions, thoughts, and perspectives that arise during the interaction.
- Search for a few solutions to the problem but allow for sufficient ripening time to determine the solution with care.
- At the end of the meeting, have each person share their biggest takeaway or learning from today, or have them answer the question, "What is your inspired action from today's meeting?"

8

THE COURAGE
TO BE PRESENT

Being human is a guest house. Every morning brings a new arrival.

—Rumi

In my mindful leadership course, I focus on working with managers on their ability to be aware, to respond to what is happening at this very moment, and to contain the unknown.

It sounds like a strange concept, but acknowledgment of the unknown is a simple, practical, and sincere consent to check and meet the reality of the moment. It is the ability to be present in the moment itself—and recognize our feelings, sensations, and thoughts—without immediately attempting to give interpretations and explanations or a solution. It's about living with discomfort and the ability to not know an immediate answer.

Why do we aim for this? Think about your average business experience. Many of us have undergone a significant change in the workplace, such as a restructuring, that involved the chance of causing considerable damage to employees' working conditions. Management teams often try to display a rosy picture, even if the reality is far from it. They tell employees that they are fighting for them to retain their jobs.

I was in a consulting role, where I was trying to mitigate exactly this type of challenge for my client.

The question presented to me was how to manage this change when it was evident to everyone that the change would significantly affect a large number of employees. The vice president I was working with was mostly concerned about senior-level employees leaving the organization if they knew too much, because the attrition would be devastating. In order to control the rollout of information, he didn't want to say anything to the employees.

I asked what he thought would be the consequences of such a move, how people would react once they received a decision in which they were not involved. He replied that he thought they would not respond well.

I suggested a different approach entirely, one in which employees would take part in the process, one based on living with the discomfort of the current mandate and reaching out to the team. We decided to create focus groups where the vice president would present everyone with the real picture—not the rosy one—and ask for their opinions. I suggested that he come to them as someone who wants to consult with them and hear their ideas or thoughts on ways to deal with the situation.

No doubt, taking on this task was not an easy thing. It required him to be in a position of not knowing. If until that moment he embodied the rescuer figure with all the answers, he was now required to come down from his pedestal and face reality.

WHAT IS PRESENCE?

Presence is developing a skill for being in the moment and experiencing everything that comes along with it.

It's a lot harder than it sounds.

Presence does not mean a person is balanced or calm. It means we are in the process of acting on opposing forces that generate energy. We are present when we change according to our experiences.

Presence requires deep listening, and a sense of openness beyond the personal perception of the thinking person. A moment of presence requires us to let go of old identities and automatic behaviors, to abandon the need for control, and to prefer choices that serve evolution in life. The importance of the present moment lies in the possibility of creating a changing new reality that is not based on past experiences and recycling existing patterns.

When we are present, we may feel that we are becoming vulnerable. This is an internal state in which our identity, which includes our perceptions, attitudes, and beliefs, doesn't have to be established. Because we do not know what will develop in dialogue and what will emerge from it, being present will enable the unknown to take place, and for changes to occur until the answer to whatever we are questioning becomes clear. It requires us to be in an emotional state that is not necessarily comfortable and pleasant for us. Sometimes it requires us to be able to experience other people's unpleasant feelings and thus to connect with the uncomfortable feelings that exist in us as well.

All of this can create a feeling of unease and a sense of weakness, even though this is not the case. We actually have to build strength to mitigate our discomfort and sit with it.

The behaviors someone with a high degree of self-awareness would demonstrate within the context of leading and managing groups include reflection and the ability to shift focus when necessary. Self-awareness is the process of investing in one's personal growth and becoming overtly conscious of how we affect the world around us. This requires time to reflect on what matters, on how our habits influence what we do and how we interact with others and understanding how we can develop our impact over time. The ability to shift focus when necessary comes as a natural consequence of that awareness, when we are clear on how we have to change and improve our reactions and how we can better plan for our future success.

EMOTIONAL INTELLIGENCE AND AWARENESS

Emotional intelligence is a key part of understanding the field in which businesses operate. There are two basic needs a person performs: task roles and social/emotional roles in groups—and they are very challenging to do at the same time. Emotional experiences give us color, meaning, and intensity to life; for this reason, many people believe that emotional and general intelligence are different. As noted by researcher Daniel Goleman,[1] emotional intelligence is the ability to monitor one's own and others' feelings and emotions, to discriminate among them, and to use this information to guide one's thinking and actions. People who understand and perceive their own emotions are better at understanding other people's body language, tone of voice, and facial expressions. Because we mirror other people's reactions, we can build a greater ability to understand ourselves and other people through the practice of emotional intelligence.

We express emotions through cultures and genders differently; we may perceive the emotions similarly, but how they are expressed can be very different because of ingrained social values and expectations. Groups are often an influencer on how we express emotions, and this can have an impact on how people perceive themselves and their roles in a company. In addition, because different parts of the brain are activated when using specific emotions, we cannot always accurately assess how we use these emotions on a day-to-day basis at work.

Other factors also come into play when it comes to human emotions. There are threats to us as human beings, such as getting laid off or health emergencies that affect our work, and we act differently when we feel lower self-worth. This means that managers have a responsibility to be aware of how employees see themselves. This social pain is connected to the thought of being excluded, and even the perception of being excluded makes it difficult for us to succeed. Nonetheless, this is why our needs for affiliation, intimacy, and power are each different and important parts of motivation at work. We need to connect with employees' ideas and values so that we can know when best to coach or counsel.

We use emotions with those around us in one way or another. Task oriented or relationship oriented? Some people have a preference. This means a number of barriers and sensitivities to and in communication processes need to be taken into account. This complexity of messages requires skill and support, which need to be congruent, descriptive, problem-oriented, validating, specific, conjunctive, owned, and supportive in order for messages to get across coherently.

At the same time, it is also true that working groups use formal ways to communicate in order to influence interdependence as they become greater in size and complexity. When one thinks about it, two people talking is a much simpler process compared to having a company try to communicate and interact. It is the structure of the group that influences the structure of the communication process in question. In addition, the flatter the feedback loops, the more opportunity for open and strategic communication. This cannot happen easily when there is a strict hierarchy in place. There is a set of behaviors and expectations for people communicating from either a place of power or the bottom of the company, for example, that can affect what people feel comfortable sharing with one another, but these are impacted by our ability to be present.

PROBLEM-SOLVING WITH PRESENCE

Two weeks after our initial meeting, I met with the vice president again. As soon as I saw him, I could sense that he was angry and that his entire entity was in resistance to the ideas we had discussed before.

He told me the process had been very hard. People were angry and frustrated with the situation. In some groups, creative solutions were offered; in others, people only released steam. He didn't believe the meetings were productive, and he was thinking of ending them.

I listened to him very carefully and nonjudgmentally. After he finished expressing his feelings, I said that I understood his discomfort. I pointed out that I had not assured him that the process would be either easy or simple but that those meetings were very significant. If he had approached the work in the opposite way, employees would be upset for different reasons, and he would have faced different hurdles. At least this way, they had been heard and some ideas were being generated.

I have to point out that during my meeting with the vice president, I felt something parallel to what he felt. Throughout the encounter he expressed his frustration and even tried to challenge my professional perceptions and disagree with me. I remember feeling that I had not fulfilled his wishes, yet I still believed everything was okay, and that his emotional response was part of the process. I had to contain the discomfort this had caused me, and I knew that his ability to unload his feelings was a necessary step toward success.

By the end of the meeting, the vice president realized that despite his discomfort, he was on the right track. Despite his ambivalence and resistance, he embraced mindfulness, the presence, the transformation; above all, he was ready to give it a chance.

In doing so, he created trust and partnership with the managers of the organization. When some of the employees were later affected by cuts, they still felt a commitment and connection to the organization. Their opinions were heard, and some of the ideas they came up with were taken into consideration. The sweeping attrition the vice president had feared did not take place.

STEP FOUR: BE AWARE AND PRESENT

We need to be aware of and create a space for attention to our emotions. Managers can work with their teams to develop a space of observation, reflection, an examination of the underlying assumptions, and at the same time a space of containment without judgment of internal or external responses to challenges. People rarely make decisions based on rational thought, no matter how hard they try to create a barrier between their emotions and their work. There is a need to engage in understanding how emotions have an effect on individuals in the workplace, especially under the normal stress and pressure of an average job. Leaders need to be aware of when and where personality clashes, as well, can get in the way of goal achievement. By decreasing the friction that emotions, personalities, and conflicts can cause, presence allows leaders to deftly create a better alignment between goals and the abilities of people to achieve those goals.

- Reflect on your assumptions. Try to challenge them and see if they still serve you or it's time to let go of them and adopt new ones.
- Don't avoid disagreements. It's okay to be afraid, but don't let fear manage you. Dare to approach friction and disagreement with an open heart and mind.
- Be proactive and take matters into your hands. If something disturbs you and doesn't feel right, act on it. Don't let life navigate the course; co-create your reality and initiate a difficult conversation when needed.
- Be opinionated. Dare to bring your voice to the workplace. Remember that you are working there for a reason. People appreciate people who are engaged and dare to show up.
- Be respectful to yourself, your peers, and employees. Even though we don't always agree with one another, when people feel you respect

them, they will respect and appreciate you, and will feel comfortable talking to you.

- Dare to be vulnerable. You don't need to know everything. When you are present and dare to not know the answer, this will provide legitimacy for others also to be vulnerable in the same way.

DEEPENING
COMPASSION
AND EMPATHY

*It is only with the heart that one can see rightly; what is
essential is invisible to the eye.*

—Antoine de Saint-Exupéry

Scott Shute, the head of Mindfulness and Compassion Programs at
LinkedIn, told me about the company's effort to act from a place of
compassion.

"Compassion is a broader issue. And right now, what interests me is to
codify this matter so that we become a compassionate company—from the
head of the company to the last one among the employees," he said.

"For example, instead of saying we want to be a ten-billion-dollar company, we're talking about how many jobs we want to produce, or how many
jobs we've found for our employees who left. We know companies that create
this magic triangle: their customers, customer needs, and employee needs.
They do this on purpose, and they are the ones that last longer and make the
most money. It's definitely a good feeling to build a thriving business and
then move on to the next level."

As Shute describes it, the average sales department vice president often
tells their salespeople that if they do not meet quotas, they will be fired.
Instead, he recommends that people talk more deeply about their corporate
values and understand customers in a compassionate way. In that way,

companies can begin to understand what customers are looking for and how their salespeople can help.

"The topic of mindfulness enters the company through meditation classes. Additionally, once a month, professional development resources are offered through visiting speakers, materials, and methods that can help drive interest in and application of mindfulness principles at work."

Shute notes that he can't keep up with demand. "In the last three years I've guided hundreds of meetings," he told me. "I held a challenging one-month event, twenty meditation sessions that lasted thirty days, and fifteen thousand people signed up."

As an individual in a leadership position, how can you show up in a compassionate way? How can you turn compassion into self-compassion?

Shute explains that at LinkedIn, only managers who treat their employees properly will keep their jobs. There is a natural selection process that separates non-compassionate people from the rest, and shows them the door.

"People treat each other better and maintain ethics standards," he explains. "This approach is based on creating a sense of community, because interpersonal relationships are necessary for today's organizations that need to be agile, flexible, and responsive to changing customer demands and promote the right things."

A sense of community is a significant component in creating a sense of belonging and meaning for employees and their desire to belong to the organization, as well as their ability to get things done.

ADVOCATING FOR COMMUNITY

Today, in a reality in which we work a significant percentage of hours in the day, people look for jobs that give them a sense of belonging and community. Employees look for a meaningful life and hope to achieve it through work. They do this by connecting with others through a social, value, and shared purpose. The ability to experience a feeling of partnership allows people to connect to something greater than themselves, to work toward a common goal, and to gain satisfaction that can lead to self-transcendence.

Leadership is important in advocating for meaning and community. A community is a place of high-quality connections. Connecting with other people evokes positive feelings and trust. And it's in relationships where we can truly see one another and our value to the community. Beyond enhancing work functionality, we can find an emotional depth in our work, as well as a sense of partnership and trust between people. An atmosphere of belonging gives employees a sense that they are part of something bigger than a large corporation.

Leaders can manifest these ideals in a culture that sees employees as a part of a holistic wholeness. This is the opposite of bureaucratic behavior—based on balanced social networks guided by a common vision and values instead of through control and command functions.

Ultimately, we must recognize that the need for belonging is inherent to human beings. If we can't, we'll disconnect from the people we need to enhance our business aims.

When we are in a workplace that supports a community atmosphere, we bestow affection on others and care for them, respond to their needs, respect them, and see them as they are. Relationships are based on caring and empathy.

GETTING TO TRUST

There is a saying that claims that while everything can be said out loud, the question is *how* to say things.

It's a saying with which I strongly agree.

The *way* we share, confront, or say what is in our hearts will make a difference in how this will resonate on the other side—whether it builds trust and partnership, harms and creates a gap, or divides and destroys trust. The ability to promote change and produce honest and authentic communication is first and foremost based on respect for ourselves and for everybody else.

The willingness to speak from the core of being without grasping for results and how exactly things will be resolved is an essential concept. This is the place that requires us to trust ourselves, our professionality, and our abilities.

Most modern work is increasingly team-based. In the last two decades, in many companies more than three-quarters of an employee's time is spent communicating with coworkers. In Silicon Valley, programmers are encouraged to work together, in part because research shows that groups tend to produce innovation faster, see mistakes more quickly, and find better solutions. Research also shows that people who work in teams tend to achieve better results and report higher satisfaction. Managers in a 2016 study reported that profitability increased as employees collaborated more closely.[1]

A cardinal part of creating an interpersonal connection is the ability to create trust and partnership-based relationships. As teamwork takes up more space and mindful leadership replaces traditional leadership, building trust-based relationships becomes a critical component of the work. We need to do this to motivate people, be it colleagues, customers, employees, or managers.

A new leadership approach also requires us to fully manifest ourselves, and to do this means we need to be able to show our weaknesses and failures and be able to be uncertain.

Why? Because when we are hesitant in business, there's a reason for it. There's a product that doesn't quite work, a tone-deaf ad campaign, or an employee who isn't fully committed to the job. To acknowledge these things allows us to change these things; we need to rely on our gut instincts and emotional responses to what seems "off" in order to set the organization in the right direction.

In most management teams, a lack of confidence and unwillingness to expose weakness means this doesn't happen. Emotions are perceived as something that has no place in the workplace, and many times we are required to play the game and show that everything is good, even though the experience is very different. People may feel confused and in need of help but be afraid to reveal that part of themselves. People focus only on the rational and logical aspects of themselves, even if this sometimes comes at the expense of finding the exact solution.

To successfully change the discourse, to show up with our strengths and weaknesses and be exposed and vulnerable, requires a certain amount of trust in ourselves and in our team members. Confidence begins when people believe they are capable of coping with the challenges they face, even if they do not know how to face them.

So, what does this look like? Mindfulness-based confidence is not the same as other pathways to personal growth.

In her book *Changing Conversations in Organizations: A Complexity Approach to Change*, Patricia Shaw explains the concept of the living present; namely, new patterns of thinking that are linked to a balance between knowing and not knowing.[2] Moving away from automatic behavior creates the opportunity to land us in this place, in which the only thing that is certain is uncertainty. The nonlinearity of the process means that new opportunities can be created without knowing all the facts about a problem. Also, sometimes it is precisely the ability to lack a clear purpose or vision that allows creativity and innovation to guide our path forward. Being able to respond to opportunities that are not necessarily directly related to our goals gives us the ability to experience new things and situations and to meet new people, to be in a position of openness and curiosity, and allow the creation of new things and opportunities that we did not think of before.

This behavior of getting out of our habits and patterns allows us to experience the world from what Buddhists call the Beginner's Mind. This describes our ability to respond to what is happening at that moment with curious eyes, and to see the world with astonishment and wonder without taking anything for granted. Using the Beginner's Mind allows us to experience small moments of magic.

If we can trust ourselves to engage our Beginner's Mind, we have all the confidence we need, because we know we have it in us to be comfortable with the uncomfortable feeling of being in a place between knowing and not knowing. This behavior requires mindfulness, meaning we can be aware and mindful to the feelings and emotions of discomfort and still not allow them to manage the situation.

As I always say, each of us is whole but imperfect. Accepting this about ourselves presents us with an opportunity to start trusting ourselves.

But to achieve any of this, we have to trust ourselves first, and then others.

PSYCHOLOGICAL SAFETY

The next step is the ability to create trust and mutual respect within a team. This kind of trust refers to the ability to know that people will keep their promises, and will not use their knowledge to hurt others in the future.

In her book *The Fearless Organization*, researcher Amy Edmondson calls this trust in a group "psychological safety."[3] She found that a group's culture involves shared perceptions held by members of the group; these perceptions can involve beliefs that support the view that the team is protected at the time of taking on interpersonal risks. Psychological safety is a sense of security that the team will not embarrass, reject, or punish anyone for speaking up.

In a project called Aristotle at Google, the company tried to test what facets of work allow teams to work well together.[4] Based on data analysis of fifty-one thousand employees, it was found that, more than anything else, psychological safety is critical to creating a situation in which the team works effectively. However, they did not know how to translate this knowledge into action. They contacted Google employees and found that the behavior that creates psychological safety requires empathy as part of the unwritten rules we apply when we need to make contact and connect. This social connection is as important at work as anywhere else, and sometimes even more important. The project taught Google that nobody wants to pretend when they come to the office. No one wants to leave parts of their personality at home. People want to express themselves and be fully present in the workplace; they want to feel free to share things that scare them without fear of accusation.

We need to be able to talk about what feels confusing, sad, and be able to have difficult conversations with colleagues whose relationships are challenging and sometimes uncomfortable. We cannot be focused solely on efficiency. When we start the morning in collaboration with a team of programmers, then send an email to our marketing colleagues, then pop in for a conference call, we want to know that the people who work with us—be it a coworker, manager, or friend—really see us as human beings. We want to know that work is more than just work. Using intensive data collection and number processing, Google reached the same conclusion that good managers have always known: In the best teams, people listen to one another and express sensitivity to the needs and feelings of others.

A beautiful illustration of this subject was outlined in a recent Simon Sinek podcast. Sinek once sat in on a meeting with a senior management team as a large consulting firm delivered a high-cost diagnostic report on their organization. The purpose of the meeting was to present the conclusions and discuss how management could take the report and implement its findings. He didn't understand what was being said, or what the company was supposed to do, but no one in the room dared to ask for clarification, presumably so as not to look like an idiot. Sinek wondered whether he should ask the question. Finally, he decided to take the risk and say that he didn't understand the report at all. To his surprise and delight, he was not the only one; to the contrary, everyone else was also confused. By asking the question, Sinek provided a service to all the managers in the room who didn't want to be the first one to raise their hand.

Is anyone among us unfamiliar with this kind of situation? In conversations with colleagues, managers, or anyone else, we may not get what they are talking about or not understand their intent. Then the question is how to respond. Of course there is no unequivocal answer as to how to proceed.

Sometimes there are situations in which authenticity means understanding that there is no place to express your perceptions right now, perhaps because of the immaturity of the people present to absorb the ideas. Also, when we dare to be authentic, we may find that other people feel as we do but don't dare to admit it. In consulting and working with groups, I find that this happens a lot. In my experience, if there is a feeling in the room, most often it is not one person's felt sense alone. A leader should be the one to ask the most difficult questions first, to provide a path forward.

GETTING FROM COMMUNITY TO COMPASSION

Compassion is a key concept in Buddhist philosophy.

To build compassion, we have to have an awareness of human suffering and the desire to find, or give, relief from it. Compassion is the recognition that failures and hardships are universal human experiences that should be welcomed rather than denied or ignored.

According to Buddhist traditions, compassion is a thought and emotion characterized by an aspiration and practical desire in which one is committed to act to alleviate the suffering of others and to help them achieve complete release from suffering. Self-compassion is choosing to act kindly to ourselves, as we would act toward a good friend. When one encounters life's difficulties or confronts personal mistakes, failures, and deficiencies, self-compassion can allow us to respond with self-kindness, recognizing that suffering is shared by all, and without self-judgment and criticism.[5]

Compassion grows from the deepest understanding that everything is connected and that our separation from one another is an illusion. It is the ability to see the imperfection of a colleague, a friend, or any person and be patient with them. It isn't just the ability to feel what another feels (which is empathy) but the ability to act, to reach out to a colleague or employee with the will to help him.

Treated with compassion, people will give of themselves, invest in their work, and be committed to their team. Once people feel that they are seen as a whole person—their feelings, thoughts, and complexity included—they will be ready to execute an action or task, even if it does not serve them personally in the short term. They will do it for the common purpose of their community at work.

Creating a sense of community requires bringing compassion into play more broadly. In order to do this, management must encourage contact, connection, communication, and interpersonal relationships.

The word "connection" is repeated all the time in organizational discourse. Through connection we can explore the positive, growing and enabling vividness in organizations, and focus on exploring positive emotions, mental health, and well-being. Being able to experience well-being through mutual compassion offers a sense of connection and a sense of contribution. This work also promotes the achievement of organizational goals through collaboration and broad vision.

In the end, compassion, and its resulting self-acceptance, offers the opposite of judgment. Letting go of our imperfections and those of others will allow us to participate fully in whatever challenges we face.

And, let's face it, a lot of things we face today show us that we are not really in control. Control is a kind of illusion that helps us deal with things that we can't control. A realistic approach is one in which we are constantly required to continue to learn, acquire new skills, try new things, sometimes succeed and sometimes not. Recognizing that we and others are human and imperfect allows us to succeed because we are facing reality.

STEP FIVE: LINK COMMUNITY AND COMPASSION

The importance of emotional connection between employees is critical for creating a sense of belonging and the ability to promote a common goal. Interpersonal skills such as compassion, empathy, and self-acceptance provide us with an enhanced ability to collaborate in dispersed and cross-organizational teams. Therefore, we need to encourage direct sociability—a relationship-based, mutually adaptive behavior that is guided by a common vision and values that encourage relationship building, sharing, and learning from one another.

Here are a few ways to start this process:

- Manage triggers. If someone triggers you, pause and try to practice compassion. Try to understand the other person's actions and the pain they themselves are holding. How can you help? Now try to understand what triggers you and try to work with it. For instance, in an uncomfortable situation, ask to set up a meeting so that you can prepare and calm yourself without being managed by anger and frustration.
- Dedicate time to the onboarding process. When an employee joins the organization, there is a certain entry process through which he or she learns about organizational processes and norms. A few weeks down the line, have a conversation with your human resources manager to learn about the employee's satisfaction in onboarding.
- Create informal meetings between leaders and new employees. Take new employees to lunch and invite them into informal conversation. This enables a deeper acquaintance and connection on a personal level.
- Give personal attention to events in employees' lives. Celebrate birthdays and holidays, and see employees as beyond their functional role in the company. Offer company events that will enable people to connect on a personal level.
- Hold informal interviews. View the candidate from different angles, informally, to understand who the person sitting in front of you truly is.

10

TRUST AS THE FOUNDATION OF SELF

He who does not trust enough will not be trusted.

—Lao Tzu

Jaden, founder of Tantalus, uses the image of a samurai to describe the way he chooses to communicate with his team. We may all be familiar with the term—a member of Japan's warring aristocracy during the preindustrial era—but what we may not know is that "samurai" actually means "to serve," representing the idea of self-transcendence.

As he told me, acting through the ideology of a samurai creates "communication which is derived from a much more balanced place, from a much more open place. An archetype of a samurai is one who works entirely from his center where he is not afraid of anything. You can communicate the bad and the good, but you do not process or share information just to please someone, entirely without vanity. I don't know if this succeeds to eliminate the ego, because the ego is always in the middle of everything, but the place of the samurai looks at the processes first, without arrogance."

In this way, Jaden believes that the ability to serve the goals of the organization and its people will be achieved through balanced communication and from the core of being open and fearless, which will bring about the inner truth.

Communicating without arrogance is a large part of this equation. Arrogance represents patronizing communication and excessive confidence that is not subject to reflection and self-examination. In contrast, Jaden follows teachings that speak of the elimination of the ego and connect this notion to humility. Humility is a trait or emotion through which we perceive ourselves as an equal among equals and seek to integrate our service into the world. That is, to be able to serve others, one must act out of humility, become mindful to inner truth, and express it without fear.

Jaden says that the ideology of a samurai is connected to a wider vision, beyond the short term and immediate results. This concept is not concerned with creating an impression or social desirability, and it is not directly connected to business results. It is parallel to the concept expressed in the complexity theory of nonlinearity known in popular terms as the "butterfly effect." The butterfly effect suggests that we have no absolute control over the outcome of any event. The samurai point of view is therefore similar to *wu wei* as discussed earlier, describing a situation in which we use the least energy possible rather than trying to control everything. This approach allows for proactivity, but at the same time it supports spontaneous behavior to emerge and grow out of action. In this way we stop being attached to one thing or another, and a foundation is formed for emergence and growth. Basically, we must free ourselves of the beliefs and perceptions we have in order to let positive outcomes emerge naturally.

The ability to act as a samurai requires the use of contradictory movements, however. In order to bring authentic inner wisdom into being, sometimes we need to go beyond fear. We must create a space for a solution to emerge, one that is formed out of interaction rather than action.

BUILDING TOWARD INTUITION

Creating a strong sense of intuition is the ultimate aim of building our self-trust.

In a business climate that looks at charts, graphs, and trends, it is often easy to overlook another aspect of existence. Many answers, solutions, and inventions lie in our subjective experience, the ebb and flow of our inner sea—a sea filled with depth, creativity, and intuition. It is in this sea of intuition that some of the greatest innovation has been born, from Apple computers to strategic decision making, in the most successful of companies.

An example of this came from one of my clients. She said she was at the crossroads of deciding whether to accept a new position. There were two proposals for her. One was more attractive in terms of economic conditions and employment security; the second was less favorable in terms of terms and wages. Her inner feeling nevertheless attracted her to the second, less-favorable offer. She finally decided to listen to her gut feeling and accept the less logical and rational proposal.

Interestingly, not too long ago it became clear that she had made the right decision. Only a few weeks after her decision, the company that was more attractive in terms of conditions was exposed to a huge loss; their stock dropped by 45 percent within seven trading days, resulting in massive lay-offs. If she hadn't followed her intuition, she would have been laid off and left without a job.

Intuition is related to emotion, and it doesn't always have a rational explanation. But at the same time, it may be linked to internal instincts with which we are picking up cues that are hidden from our other senses.

Take Susan Gillis Chapman's example from her book *The Five Keys to Mindful Communication*.[1] She describes a man in Alaska working in the kitchen with his dog tied up outside of the house. Through the kitchen window, the man saw a bear coming toward the house. In a fit of anguish, he realized he couldn't save his dog from the approaching bear. Stunned, the man stood and watched as his dog wagged its tail at the bear's arrival. The bear happily responded to the dog's delight, and they played together. For years, the bear continued to visit and play with the dog. The dog reacted from an instinctual rather than a cognitive place, an emotional place. He knew the bear wasn't a threat.

Likewise (but especially when we're not under a threat like a wild bear or a raging CEO) we can also learn to connect with these instincts, understand something greater about those around us and about what is possible.

Janice Marturano, in her book *Finding the Space to Lead*, claimed that mindful leadership is the ability to be connected to oneself, to the other, and to the wider community.[2] The connection to community comes from the ability to see the bigger picture larger than the self. Connecting to the self means being mindful to our gut feelings and emotions and giving them space and expression as opposed to alienation, fragmentation, and even detachment. Seeing beyond means looking beyond logic and rational thought as well as connecting to the heart, to the stomach, to what is inside us at every level of conscious and unconscious awareness.

In *A Taste of Irrationality: Predictably Irrational and Upside of Irrationality*, Dan Ariely explains how our judgment is biased by expectations, emotions, social norms, and added forces—invisible and irrational—and claims we are underestimating the impact of emotion in our decision making.[3] Solving problems is obviously a desired trait in the business world. However, most people do this only with the intellect and rational mind. We also must develop trust in our intuition and in ourselves before we can discover the motivation to overcome obstacles of any significance.

Biased judgment and decision making decreases the ability of an individual to consider all the options open to them in order to benefit their work and, therefore, to mindfully shift.[4] It's important for us to consider alternative explanations to the ones in our own head, anchors we're carrying, possible outcomes, perspectives, and countervailing evidence. We need to consider potential situational influences on our behavior, as well as the ability to balance perceived rules and options to change the status quo, but the reality is that we don't when we're constrained by a business ethos that rejects the fluidity and adaptability that comes naturally to us as people.

HONING OUR CONSCIOUS THOUGHT ADVANTAGE

Our intuition, as defined by social psychologists, is based on large numbers of patterns gained through experience, resulting in different forms of underlying knowledge, knowledge we don't think about all the time.[5] This definition of intuition suggests that experts need to acquire thousands of patterns. These patterns are not generic tools; they are specific accumulations of direct and vicarious experiences.

At the heart of it, every decision we need to make is a point at which we can get curious and make an intentional change, and we can do it consciously or unconsciously. Research tells us that by bringing attention to where we can grow our awareness, we can create what's called a "conscious thought advantage," which helps us thrive in life. We can develop the skill to make self-aware, effective, and conscious decisions. A conscious thought advantage still uses our tacit, learned knowledge, but it allows us to play with options in a way that creates new energy around decision making. Developing these skills in this way is about building conscious awareness about why we do the things we do so that we choose a path that is right for us rather than one we expect to follow.

Think about the choice to run a yellow light. There are probably several dozen considerations at stake in the car and around us. Is it an empty rural road or an urban environment? Is it a matter of conventionally turning left on a yellow in the midst of traffic? Hitting the intersection just as the green turns yellow, or rushing to get to the line just as it's going to turn red? Do we just want to run the light for some reason we've justified to ourselves? Chances are, no matter the variables, we make a split-second decision on a yellow light that doesn't register unless something goes wrong that changes the rest of our day.

Researchers tell us that these kinds of split decisions don't always register with us for a reason: Our brains have, quite literally, the ability to drive our cars even when we're not aware of doing it. We all have a set of brain structures called the "default mode network"; it's something even newborns have. A series of studies at the Universities of Cambridge and York in the United Kingdom have shown that once we learn how to do something, such as playing a game or driving a car, our brains allow us to do those tasks without consciously thinking about them.[6] In fact, the same research indicates that when we act in default mode more often (and we can actually learn how to train our own default mode), we can make better choices in general rather than just for the subconscious decisions connected to typical default mode activities. In fact, self-awareness plays a role in managing the balance between default and conscious decisions to our advantage.[7] The default mode's role in self-awareness—or, in practical terms, reflection on what we do and what matters to us—makes it useful in consolidating and using our memories.

Strengthening intuition means building experiences that result in more accurate and comprehensive tacit knowledge. Strengthening intuition means accelerating expertise within the default mode in our neurological systems. In other words, when we master our conscious decisions and build certain skills into that mode of operating, we can spend more time focusing on what we'd like to focus on and building toward contentment and success at work. When we master our conscious decisions and are more aware of the shifts we make, we snap out of what once was autopilot and take the driver's seat.

PLAYING CARDS

An interesting study linking decision making, body, sensations, and intuition showed just how this works.[8] Researchers asked participants to play a card game. Each received an initial two-thousand-dollar cash amount, and their goal was to make as much money as possible in the game in order to win. But the game was biased in advance. There were four playing card decks, each with either a red or a black logo.

The researchers planted cards in each deck that created higher risks or higher rewards for those playing. In the deck of cards with a black logo, however, there were fewer risks involved and fewer rewards. They were safer. Although you wouldn't make as much money, there were very limited ways in which to lose money. In order to win in the long run, participants had to pick cards from the black deck.

Participants began to play. After fifty rounds they were asked which pack of cards would be the one they believed was most likely to win the game. Since they had no direct knowledge of where the higher or lower risk or reward cards were actually placed, only a felt sense of what was happening, they could only say what their gut instinct was. After only ten rounds of play, their palms had sweated when they went to pick up cards from the red packs. But after eighty rounds, they had started to figure out what was going on.

This indicates that our bodies have wisdom that we cannot always rationally explain. Sometimes when faced with a decision, we know from within; we experience a kind of "knowing" about the right decision, but it takes time to explain it logically and rationally to ourselves and to others.

The same gut feelings and intuitions can sometimes be pure sensations and signify the right way to act; however, sometimes those gut feelings and intuitions are not clear and can mislead us and cause confusion. We may access our automatic patterns, which can lead to a decision based on fear, without being fully present and responding to what is happening here and now. There is room to give space and respect to gut feelings, but it is also necessary to stop and pay attention to what they represent, what they are meant to tell us. Is our concern justified?

Strengthening our intuition creates cognitive flexibility so that we can work to our advantage. A strong intuition allows us to be creative; it allows us to move through social situations with more ease and allows us to access our learned information. It makes us more self-aware. Increasing intuition can help us feel like experts so that we are confident in trusting what we already know so that we're ready to shift, ready not to fail. So part of the mindfulness practice is just that: practicing using our intuition, or at least listening to it a bit more. Trusting ourselves to be our own experts at being *us*.

That doesn't mean we're always going to be right, or that our gut feeling is always going to lead us in the right direction. But we can begin to be reflective and honest about where we're usually right, where we're probably right, and where we need more information.

Mindful behavior is the ability to be connected to these feelings and become aware of what really matters. It's important that we understand just how much trusting ourselves, and others, matters to the workplace. We must be willing to remove the blocks to our inner wisdom and intuition so that we may recognize and experience the truth of the situation we are in, and who we can become. When we don't trust ourselves, we remain in bad relationships where we are not trusted in return, wrecking our self-esteem. We work harder in jobs where we aren't valued and won't ever get ahead, creating layers of physical and mental strain that may never abate. We blame others for our "bad luck" instead of being mindful so that we can try something different.

We need to value and include intuition in our work world and encourage the intuition of other people and respect their truth. This is part of effective leadership. A common misconception is that success is something we get only after we meet the right people, or when life is most always going our way. We must first develop a deep trust within ourselves—including the courage to follow our intuition even when it may go against the tide of what others may approve of—before true and full success can consistently take root and blossom.

STEP SIX: CREATING CONFIDENCE

Trust in the workplace and within ourselves is important, but few understand what this means. When we are trusting, our intuition, thoughts, and outer actions are in accord: We live in harmony with ourselves, with others, and with our environment. As I see it, three key elements are needed to create trust: empathy, authenticity, and vulnerability. All these elements require us to check in with our intuition.

Empathy is the ability to sense where the people on the other side of the table are at, what bothers them, and what their needs are. How can we increase empathy?

- Encourage and strive for processes to be formed through contact and direct communication, which encourages employees to promote interpersonal relationships based on connection and compassion.
- Create opportunities for nonrational learning experiences based on emotions and emotional connection between people. Allow people to know each other more broadly and prioritize feelings and emotions.
- Encourage self-management. This preserves intimate personal connection with work, and preserves aspiration. Allow employees to define formal boundaries among them through listening and empathy.

Authenticity is the ability to dare to be true to our values and perceptions and act according to them based on our own truth. To dare to be in areas of disagreement and not please others just in order to avoid conflict. How can we increase authenticity?

- Dare to listen to our emotions. Usually our gut feelings want to tell us something.
- Practice meditation each day, even for just a few minutes. This helps us become more connected to our inner life, our sensations, feelings, and emotions. Find what works best for you. It can be a walking meditation, sitting meditation, body scan, mantra meditation, and much more.
- Try to understand what your gut feeling is telling you. If you feel that part of you is scared, try to understand why. Is it scared because making a decision will push you out of your comfort zone? Or is it a red light telling you something is not right about this decision?
- Be loyal to your own thoughts and feelings. We often embrace belief systems that are not ours and then live according to them instead of our own beliefs.
- Walk the talk, and act according to your belief system.

- Keep promises and deliver on time, and be transparent if you aren't able to deliver on time.
- Learn to set boundaries from an assertive place. It's OK to say no. By learning to put boundaries in place, you respect yourself and others.

Vulnerability is the ability to express in our own voices, even in situations where we have no coherent answer. We must learn to expose the experience of confusion and unknowing and agree to not know all the answers. We also need to learn to demonstrate weaknesses that exist in us and the places where we need help. How can we increase vulnerability?

- Be courageous and reveal your true colors.
- Come from a position of learning; ask questions and explore.
- Dare to say that you don't know the answer and ask for help when you need it.
- Nourish a nonjudgmental culture. Let people feel comfortable being vulnerable with you and in meetings. Appreciate this kind of communication, and acknowledge that it is challenging.
- Enable a culture of trial and error, and give legitimacy to mistakes.

11

GRATITUDE TO ALL

There is a battle of two wolves inside us all. One is evil. It is anger, jealousy, greed, resentment, lies, inferiority, and ego. The other is good. It is joy, peace, love, hope, humility, kindness, empathy, and truth. The wolf that wins? The one you feed.

—Cherokee Proverb

Michael was considering a request from a senior employee at Tantalus.

"Next year he wants to move to London," Michael said. "I offered him some jobs, but leaving this office could mean that he would have to step back professionally. Because of that, he searched for a new job on his own in London and found one. I'm happy that he's found a place that seems appropriate for him. He has been here for nine years, from the beginning, but I think he is doing the right thing. It's healthy for him and, in a sense, healthy for our company."

The last part of that story might seem like an odd thing to say.

In every case where an employee moves on, it's likely a good thing for that employee, but it's rare that a company sees this kind of change in the same light. Realistically, it's a loss, especially with someone who was part of the team from the beginning. Knowledge, experience, and community all are affected when a valued team member moves on.

But Michael looked beyond the narrow, functional viewpoint of the organization and saw the employee's need to develop and continue on his own professional path. The management team cooperated with the employee's request and tried to maintain the necessary tension between control and release of control. On one hand, the employee looked for suitable options within the company and agreed to be present within the uncertainty of the situation; on the other he was given leeway to look further afield.

In a place of gratitude and acceptance, both parties moved on.

In this case, Michael's perception of the departure of his employee was based on a holistic, long-term conceptualization of human resources: If an employee is not a good fit for the company, it would be better for them to move on to an organization where they would be satisfied so that the current organization can recruit someone who suits it better. In this way, there is an alignment between the needs of the individual and the needs of the organization.

Gratitude for what is, rather than control of what cannot be, is the foundation of the success of the employer-employee relationship.

As Michael explains, "One of the things I talk about with the managers is why it's not so bad to let someone go. The place I come from is not how the company can make a few more pennies. Focusing on money alone lowers the whole team; it makes the whole team work harder because of the force it creates. Letting someone go, whether through attrition or layoffs or firing, doesn't necessarily mean the person or the company is a failure; it's just a mismatch, and it may or may not be able to be fixed."

GRATITUDE FOR FAILURE

Michael is right. We can't learn without failure. We have to move toward expertise by doing, trying, and failing. We can identify what makes us content, what inspires us; we can be conscious and present about what's happening around us, and then we can make shifts when and where we know them to be necessary.

For example, getting fired is perceived as a negative and unpleasant experience, at least in the short term. That's because the experience involves harming one's ego, visibility, and perception of oneself as a part of a certain group of people. On one hand there is a need to set a boundary, to break up and confront the employee for the benefit of both parties; on the other there is a desire to avoid ending the relationship that is characterized by dragging feet that can cause hurt on both sides. But creating gratitude around saying goodbye can enable an employee to find a better job, which can increase his quality of life and job satisfaction and enable him to develop and be empowered. The company can also discover what it liked about that employee and show gratitude for his service, while at the same time exploring what a new person or role might add to the equation. At the same time, we cannot set aside the fact that there are growing pains to manage. Employees who are left behind may feel at risk of their own dismissal. Mindful leaders can help both the employees who leave and those who stay behind to deal with this uncertainty.

Experts call this process of trying and failing naturalistic decision making, something that's been studied for decades but hasn't quite made it into the mainstream. It's about intentionally developing an interest in trusting your own judgment and building intuition skills so that you can shift naturally, in alignment with who you are and what you're trying to move toward in life. Looking at the experiences of mountaineers who are top performers in making decisions under duress in a group, leading American researchers in the field of organizational psychology found that perseverance is not an optimal response.[1] If a group of people continually push one another to their limits, it leads not only to insufficient rest but also a willingness to persist while injured, leading to more injury as well as mental strain. It's a causal loop, and perseverance under pressure results in really poor decision making. Instead, we can strengthen our intuition by creatively predicting what might happen.

Of course, we want to feel our passions and follow a path of least resistance. We want to follow our passions because we want to be happy, and we never want to fail. We want to have success as we ourselves define it. But what I learned from working with companies and leaders who are mindful is that passion can come from more than one source. It can come from hundreds or thousands of sources. Instead of trying to follow our passions, we should find the things that make us feel passionate every day, at every moment we can.

Gratitude, even in failure, begets an emotional language of containment and support: farewell, humanness, a final embrace; words that represent contact, proximity, and interpersonal connection; empathy for the other; and behavior characterized by emotional and social intelligence that sees beyond the self.

Gratitude, therefore, sometimes requires the same kind of awareness and courage that we've been discussing all along. In this case, Michael indicated that he chose to allow the employee a respectable departure as opposed to the usual conduct in an organization based on a fear of loss or money. This approach required courage. Michael had to trust the employee and their relationship, and he had to trust in the belief that it would not hurt the company.

UNDERSTANDING THE POWER OF GRATITUDE FOR INCREASING HUMAN ENGAGEMENT

Gratitude creates a basis for good interpersonal relationships through the establishment of norms of respect and a positive regard for the needs and contributions of everyone in a company. It helps develop a connection between people that is beyond the self through thankful discourse and the ability to acknowledge what others have achieved, as well as what teams have achieved together.

"Gratitude," as a psychological term, is a sense of miracle and appreciation for life. In companies it allows employees to learn from their successes and to see the glass half full. It gives employees a sense of value, hope, and optimism; it encourages the spirit of doing and even enables them to act out of love and commitment to change and growth. It's the opposite of taking employees for granted, which can cause a sense of worthlessness, frustration, and disrespect. That's why cultivating gratitude is important for increasing employee engagement in organizations—because of its direct impact on organizational climate improvement and its contribution to reciprocity in relationships.

Without gratitude, advancing in true success will not occur.

Gratitude is the attitudinal password that takes you through the doorway to a work world where the glass is always half full.

Gratitude isn't only about saying thank-you, either. It's about recognition.

As one employee at Tantalus told me, "I think people are very flattering here and give feedback on a personal level, saying it out loud. Occasionally they will give a weekend voucher and announce it at the company level, but the prize is not what matters here. I think it's mostly important for people to know that management is satisfied with them."

As another put it, "There was great pressure to release some product, and everyone complained a lot about the product quality. Michael and Jaden talked with us. We were pushed; we felt it was a mission of the company and we had better improve quality. But these conversations stressed the importance of what we do in the company. It's not that if you don't succeed then and there you'll be fired. It's about this positive assessment of our worth that spurs us on. You sit with your manager, and he really tells you that you've got the team on track. It's fun, and it's not only in appraisal sessions that you get this kind of feedback, even during work itself. I think it is important for everyone because the work here is tough. And that kind of stuff lifts you up when needed."

A culture of appreciation is expressed in the ability to correct mistakes and recognize successes. This creates shared meaning with employees through their connection to seeing the broader picture.

LinkedIn does this as well. As Scott Shute says, "Take, for example, the team meetings we have on Mondays. We communicate gratitude with the word 'Kudu.' You give Kudu—a beat—to your colleague, and so you both go out satisfied. There are two things that come out of this process: We learn about each other, and we strengthen the bond as we both share our gratitude. This is how each team meeting opens."

Gratitude creates a sense of value, joy, and affection and makes people give back what they receive. It lets people know they are seen, and that their contribution is valuable.

Gratitude, in this way, affects everything that is happening. It is similar to a stone thrown into the water and producing ripples. Once you have a place for positive, reassuring, grateful discourse, it can spread throughout the organization.

FINDING THE PERSONAL SPACE FOR GRATITUDE
RATHER THAN DISAPPOINTMENT

When I started writing this book, I wanted to interview a senior executive who leads a global company. Part of his agenda is connecting business and peacemaking. One morning when I was on my way to a meeting, I made a few phone calls, trying to get in contact with him. When I arrived at the meeting, I told one of my colleagues about it. It turned out that a good friend of hers was his personal assistant. I talked to her and sent her material about me and the book I was writing. She told me that her boss was very busy and would try to get in contact within a few months. A few months later, he was still too busy to connect. This pattern repeated several times.

At one point, a friend who had served with me in the army told me he worked closely with this executive, and even gave me the number of his private phone.

I swallowed my pride and sent him a message. Again, the call went unanswered. I didn't really care about his lack of cooperation personally, but I wanted to gain insight into his worldview so that I could write about it in a book and readers could be inspired by it. It just didn't seem like it was meant to be.

During this time, I traveled to a conference in Hong Kong, where I met David Yeung, whom you've read about in previous chapters. I decided to interview him instead. I liked David, and I was grateful for his time and insight.

In the final stages of writing the book, a friend sent me a newspaper article that made me even more grateful. The article reported that the man I'd never had a chance to interview was being investigated by the Securities and Exchange Commission for providing insider information. Apparently, his focus on connecting business and peacemaking wasn't enough to keep him from acting unethically.

When I read this, I immediately understood. There was probably a reason I couldn't catch him.

This story is a great illustration of how to know when our grip on control should be released, and when we should turn to gratitude for the opportunities that we can make happen for ourselves. Our goal is to pay attention. The road is embedded with signs, and it's our role to be mindful and observe what the right action truly is.

Having agreed at some point to loosen my attachment to control, I found my gratitude and found my way forward.

STEP SEVEN: ATTITUDE FOR GRATITUDE

How would your experience of yourself and your work change this instant if you stopped looking exclusively at all the obstacles and problems and instead put some of your energy into asking for new opportunities, welcoming them with gratitude, and humbly asking for more each day?

Many workplace environments have a culture of complaining, focusing on what is wrong and why you can't do something. Instead, develop an attitude of gratitude, focusing on what is right, no matter how small, and what the potential and possibilities are. This will bring more success and fulfillment into your career than complaining ever will.

Being thankful every day for the small things at work makes good things happen when you need them most. Your capacity in the workplace to give and support, respect other views, and be compassionate is your guarantee that a positive outcome to all situations is possible.

So, start with practicing your state of mind.

- Every morning be thankful for three things in your life. It can be your family, friends, projects, anything you appreciate. Don't take anything for granted. Shift your attention to positive things. Or, over dinner with your family, have everybody say one thing from today that they appreciate.
- Make it a routine to compliment someone, whether a colleague, friend, or family member.
- Encourage a grateful culture. In each meeting acknowledge an individual or a team for a job they have done and succeeded at.
- Create an Appreciation Box. Each time someone wants to appreciate a colleague, they can drop a note in the box that is announced at the next meeting.
- Acknowledge the process and the investment people are putting in. Even if it's a challenging time, amplify the good. Moreover, try to see

and show others the opportunities that connect them to the broader picture.

- Embrace appreciative inquiry in learning from success instead of from failures. Give praise to employees for the capabilities and benefits they bring to the table.

⑫

BUILDING SPACE

Silence is essential. We need silence, just as much as we need air, just as much as plants need light. If our minds are crowded with words and thoughts, there is no space for us.

—Thích Nhất Hạnh

Yaara, a Tantalus employee, told me, "From the first moment I came in—you must have felt it too—the office felt really 'wow,' but a calm wow. There's a lot of air here, and a lot of light even though it's closed off from outside."

Nathaniel agreed. "It's not the material things that create the sense of freedom, fun, and commitment, but rather the space that creates the possibility to breathe, take in air, relax. Some air, it's something we need."

About a decade ago Tantalus created a meditation room as a symbol of the importance of space in human life. The ability to be able to go somewhere to breathe quietly and connect to one's own inner peace and tranquility was of central importance to the company because it created an atmosphere of calmness, a place for being, and space. Jaden stated that the meditation room served as a spinal column for establishing the place. The spinal column metaphor acknowledges the part of the human body that makes room for stability. At the same time, the spine needs a certain amount of flexibility that will allow a person to move.

The room does not take up much space in terms of its physical dimensions, but it provides space for stability and flexibility for all employees if and when they need it.

While I was in the organization, the company was in the process of growing and expanding and, due to a rapid increase in office density, the room temporarily became a space for Jaden's secretary. But as soon as possible, the room was repurposed as a fun room. Pillows and cots were placed on the floor, a TV and electronic games were installed, massages were offered. While the original meditation room concept created a space where people could pause and disengage from work for a time, gather, and from there promote authentic communication, the message in recreating the space as a fun room seems similar. In stopping and disengaging from outside noise, employees are able to refresh their thoughts and enter into a quieter environment that brings about reflection and promotes creative thinking through play.

In this case, freedom is expressed in the creation of a space that brings into the room—physically and metaphorically—air, daylight, space, peace, and quietness. There is a sense of respect for the space because of what it offers to the Tantalus team. Space leads to abundance, infinity, unlimited possibilities. Freedom and the possibility to connect with spaciousness, air, and light are a connection to abundance.

A key practice of leadership today is giving people room to realize themselves, room to deliver creative ideas and innovation.

Without giving yourself times of stillness and quiet on a regular basis, your mind will not be clear at work and your decisions and perceptions will be clouded. People who are too busy, overstressed, and take no time for stillness tend to become faultfinders at work. They always see what is wrong and rarely see creative solutions. People who take time for quiet reflection tend to be more able to respond effectively to challenges that arise.

I once heard this beautiful analogy: When people are standing on an open roof on a high floor, as long as there is no guardrail to protect them, they will not approach the edge nor be truly free to explore the roof or even look at the view. But once there is a guardrail that protects them and creates a frame, people will go to the edge of the roof and not be afraid to fall. This is so true. Where we feel protected and guarded, when we have the psychological safety to be who we are, then we dare to try new things, manifest ourselves, even take ourselves to the edge.

In order to enable employees to realize themselves, to dare to grow, to change and take themselves to the edge, we need to allow them space to get there in their own way. We can make room for action while protecting and supporting employees.

SPACE AS AN ENABLER

A primary way to enable space is by creating a physical space in the organization that can enable more communication and casual conversations between people.

Let's look at the design of a workplace. Many workplaces, such as high-tech companies or office buildings that offer designed spaces for rent, shape the workplace in an invested way. Most of the design reflects lightness, play-fulness, and colorfulness, with the aim of influencing the atmosphere of the workplace and employees' experience. Also, many of these designs include large spaces—shared spaces where people can sit down to eat together, fun rooms, seating areas, and more.

While there are financial considerations in designing a workplace, pay attention to companies you like to enter and ones in which you like to stay. Organizations whose space is designed spaciously, that offer a clean design or have a cozy feeling, may impart implicit ideas about the company's culture. Office design also influences people's being, feelings, and actions.

Of course, you can also look at space critically.

Some companies invest in designing the workspace to create specific conditions. Benefits for employees such as gyms, dining services, babysitting, and laundry can produce normative control—namely, a set of unwritten expectations that assume that employees are going to be constantly available. This can transform the organization into a totalitarian place that meets all the needs of its employees, thus controlling their time and compelling them to stay in the workplace twenty-four hours a day, seven days a week.

Instead, think about creating a space that allows people to grow within themselves and within the company organically. In the calm and space created, employees can find inspiration and even feel a sense of meaning and influence, in the same way that some people claim their best time to get creative ideas is during their morning shower, a place of relative silence and isolation.

High-tech companies such as Check Point, Natural Intelligence, Aetna, and others offer meditation rooms for their employees. In 2016 Salesforce CEO Marc Benioff consulted Zen master Thích Nhất Hạnh to build Mindful Zones on each floor of their San Francisco offices. Benioff claims that these quiet meditation areas are very important in fostering creativity, and the fact that his company mustered $12.77 billion in assets and nearly $52 billion in sales last year shows that his approach may be working.[1]

Creating space is also about creating space in our schedules.

When I work with managers, I advise them to make an appointment with themselves during the week, a time for them not to be too busy and where they are not available to constantly extinguish fires. Managers always need to think strategically about developing new products and promoting new ideas, and of course they need to make time for that, but they also need to take time to regroup and let ideas land. Otherwise, they are so busy implementing short-term plans that they don't think deeply about the important things that require time.

Sometimes a CEO sees taking a break and sitting outside in a meeting with himself to stop and think as a waste of time and counterproductive. But making room for thought and reflection enables important issues and creative ideas to emerge.

Most people want to feel purpose in their work, but they make the mistake of only looking to the workplace for answers. Many great discoveries have been made while taking a walk in nature or even dreaming. Within the ordinary occurrences of nature, the path to purpose in your work can be found: the scent of pine in the forest, your bare feet on sun-drenched white sand, an expanse of green grass blowing in a summer breeze as you lean back to watch wisps of white clouds dance across the sky, looking out your window to see the stars sparkling across the expanse of the universe.

In our busy work world, it is easy to become part of the problem and not take the time to treat ourselves and others with respect and value. Devoting time each day for being still and "not doing" is a prerequisite for creating an effective work life with clarity of vision.

CONTROL AND LETTING GO

One of the tensions managers now face is the tension between short-term results and long-term vision. An organization that is only engaged in the short term and does not invest resources for long-term strategic thinking—where they want to go, what is happening in the market—is likely to find itself irrelevant within a few years.

We have to create space to let go of control.

It is essential to true success, and to our planetary survival, to realize that controlling other people and dominating the environment will not lead to what we want. Being humble in the workplace is something that does not get discussed much, if at all. One central attitude that comes from being humble is respect: respect for life, respect for one another, and respect for the challenges in life that allow you to grow. Humility comes from seeing the magnificence of life. Humility results from knowing you are a part of this magnificence, not apart from it. When we are humble, we let go of the idea that we can control everything around us; we end up creating space for growth.

Many organizations have assimilated this concept. At Google, for example, a procedure has been introduced that addresses the company's distribution of resources. When Eric Schmidt was CEO at Google, he went beyond their initial "Don't be evil" rule and instituted the 70-20-10 ratio for innovation. It works pretty simply:

- 70 percent of employees' time should be dedicated to core business tasks.
- 20 percent of time should be dedicated to projects related to the core business.
- 10 percent of time should be dedicated to projects unrelated to the core business.

At least 10 percent of the work being done at Google is wholly unconnected to employees' job titles or responsibilities. The company built in space specifically to allow for this freedom.

Every quarter at Twitter, employees get a whole week where they can do whatever they want. They can learn new skills, develop a new product, or anything else related to personal and collective enrichment.

CHAPTER 12

Tantalus created an innovation program in which they rewarded people for thinking outside the box, beyond boundaries and job definition, and beyond the limits of creativity.

In order to enable creative and innovative ideas to develop, ones that will make the organization innovative, it is necessary to consciously create space for it and to build mechanisms that enable people to do what feels right for them. The ability to act out of curiosity and openness may engender new knowledge and allow creativity and innovation to emerge.

If you knew your time was limited, how would you be with the people around you today, this month, this year? For most of us, the answer includes loving more deeply, expressing more gratitude, forgiving completely, and consistently being helpful when we can. These four actions can become the foundation for a successful and rewarding career, no matter what our vocation. Many people spend far more time struggling with getting more instead of taking the time to pause and give what they can, even though this is precisely what will make their work become smooth and less effortful.

Giving space to the self and being willing to be in a state of not knowing allows different voices to exist and new knowledge and wisdom to emerge. But this kind of communication requires us to be in a position of openness and curiosity, and to agree to halt for a moment the firm grasp of the righteousness or willingness of personal perceptions. It invites us to create a space for deeper observation and listening, thus connecting with the broader picture and allowing the best solution to emerge, even though it may not be the solution we initially thought would work. Ultimately, mindfulness instills in us a new sense of belonging, meaning, creativity, and compassion in all aspects of life.

Letting go of control means giving employees space and freedom of action to bring their uniqueness into play with their work. The post-bureaucratic organization has no clear boundaries, which is seen as one of the factors driving individuals to express their potential and individuality. Employees must develop their own rules and learn to integrate them in their own unique style. Creating space enables self-management, being mindful, and being present and responding to changing needs, and in this space, management cannot dictate to employees how to behave.

Shared control enables both personal and organizational control. Personal control is reflected in the fact that employees are empowered and can influence the work processes that require them to manage their emotions and relationships. Organizational control is achieved through existential empowerment, through which employees bring their personal ways of work to the organizational space.[2]

STEP EIGHT: CREATE SPACE FOR MINDFULNESS

When we act from a space created for mindfulness, we can manage ourselves in a better way by being able to pause and be present with the unknown and the discomfort. And from this place we enable new creative and innovative solutions to emerge.

When you see that finding the best solutions and being able to be in the present moment are inseparable, you begin to function at a much higher level. There is always something that seems pressing and important at work, but remember the bigger picture: Nothing can be more important in any given moment than peace of mind.

Many people believe that the more hours they spend at work, the more productive and successful they will be. However, you must take time to nurture and care for yourself, and those who work for or with you, if you are to find balance and a kind of success that will bring you anything of lasting value. Devoting time each day for being still and "not doing" is a prerequisite for creating an effective work life with clarity of vision.

Being all that you can be at work is *not* something that begins with doing or achieving something of great magnitude. Being all you can be begins with discovering that there is a grace that permeates our life, and we have to make space for it.

What does this look like?

- Find a time to nourish yourself. This can involve practicing meditation, a hobby that you like, going out into nature, meeting friends, or any other activity that refuels you.
- Create a meditation/pause routine between meetings. Put at least a five-minute break in your diary between meetings. Use this time to pause and breathe.

- Once in a while, pause to reflect and ask yourself: *Am I on the right path? Am I satisfied with my life: personal, professional, relational?*
- Measure employees by output rather than method, and allow them to achieve results in their own way. Of course, you can give general guidelines, but allow employees to bring their own unique way of solving the issue to the table.
- Create physical space in the company where people can rest, disconnect from the work, and connect to themselves. This can be a meditation room, a fun room, a balcony, or some other dedicated space.
- Create space for employees to bring various parts of themselves to the workplace and share with their colleagues. This can be a lecture about a hobby, facilitating a meeting, etc. If people like to take photos, arrange an exhibition where they can share their pictures.

13

HOLDING TENSION

As you start to walk out on the way, the way appears.

—Rumi

More than a decade ago, I worked with a team of consultants for one of the largest banks in Israel.

We met with the management team and created a process, getting a group of veteran managers together to plan for some organizational changes. I should note that before I started working there, the executive-in-charge told me that the group included one very disgruntled manager, and that if I had trouble working with him, I should remove him from the process. I immediately understood who this person was. The first day of the workshop, he offered only offensive, cynical, and unpleasant comments. Every activity we did was met with refusal and a lack of cooperation.

At the end of the day, I went home feeling very uncomfortable. I realized that this manager was probably frustrated by his work in the organization, and perhaps he was hurt by the fact that those around him had not recognized his needs. Knowing this did not ease my feeling of unpleasantness. I thought about what to do the next day and told myself that I would not continue in the same way. Getting this manager out of the workshop was not the right thing to do either. What would all my work be worth if I failed to deal with that manager and gave up on him?

I decided to go back to the group the next day and be honest. I would put the topic on the table and talk about the unpleasantness and disrespect I had experienced.

The next morning, before we started the planned day, I told the participants that I wanted to share with them my experience and the feelings with which I had ended the previous day. I mentioned that I was very hurt by the attitude of some of them and the cynical comments thrown at me. I said I felt disrespected, stating that I really hoped they would not permit anyone to behave the way they had behaved toward me yesterday.

I needed a lot of courage to do what I did—to be authentic and to talk about it. I needed courage because I didn't really know how the participants would respond to my putting myself in a place of vulnerability. But I decided that if I didn't do it, the whole process would be insignificant. It was better to risk that it would not succeed than to continue the way things had been the day before without reflecting on it. It was clear that if I chose to continue down the business-as-usual road without relating my experience, I would in a sense re-create the difficult experience. I would have legitimized and encouraged their behavior, and would not have fulfilled the role for which I was being paid.

Authentic and open communication requires emotion and personal narrative—that is the essence of mindfulness. It requires both being attuned to the emotions I am experiencing at this moment and responding to the situation without judging and hurting others. Of course we are not responsible for others' responses, but sincerity is key. By listening to my feelings, I could also be mindful and empathetic.

It is important to want to respond compassionately to all situations. When this is your goal, you look for reasons to see a positive future rather than find fault based on the past. When having an ongoing difficult situation with someone at work, ask yourself, *What experiences or suffering could this person have gone through in their life that would lead them to this act?*

Also, in stating that I hoped that participants did not allow anyone to treat them as abusively as I had been treated, I modeled a behavior and conveyed a message that this was my boundary—that I was not willing to accept their abuse. Coming from a place of sharing my personal experience, I did not call for antagonism but allowed the people in the room, who had probably experienced such abuse themselves during their work at the bank, to understand, be empathetic, and even empathize with me.

Amazingly, the group did not respond cynically or sarcastically.

We continued the activity, and they divided into groups. I was prepared for the same disgruntled and uncooperative manager to hold firm and did not expect him to participate actively. But much to my surprise, he was fully committed to participating and even took on key roles in leading the various missions. It was amazing to see the 180-degree change expressed through full cooperation, commitment, and a sense of belonging, all in such a short time.

The executives were surprised at this outcome and asked what I had done with the manager in question. My answer was that I hadn't done anything special, only seen him as he truly was. I realized that the significant change in this manager was due to the way I was acting: I was authentic about my feelings and empathetic toward his feelings. I was able to feel that manager's pain and frustration without judging his behavior, and able to connect with the broad picture, realizing that his behavior was not necessarily related to anything I had done. I realized he was probably so battered and frustrated by his own managers' attitude toward him that he was getting his frustration out.

There appears to be a need in the workplace to reduce everything to right or wrong rather than developing an open mind and a desire to understand different perspectives and approaches. The environment suffers when the interconnectedness of life is overlooked. Similarly, our work world suffers when we do not see how interconnected each person is.

For this reason, we have to be able to hold tension: the tension between the person and their work, between our interests and those of others, and between conflict and eventual resolution.

CONNECTING OPPORTUNITIES AND ABILITIES IN PRESENCE

In my experience, there is often a rational, logical, and causal discourse in organizations that not only excludes emotional discourse but leaves no room for it. This kind of behavior creates frustration plus stagnation. In the end, we are human beings who go through experiences and contain emotions;

when we express ourselves only through rational, logical, cold language—solely analytical perception—nothing can change.

In many business conversations, someone says, "Let's start with the facts." But facts are just part of the story. Unlike smart machines, we feel, we experience, and these emotions paint our subjective experience. There is really no absolute truth based on facts; everyone sees things through their personal prism, which is colored by their own emotions, thoughts, and feelings. Hence, two people can be in the same situation but experience reality as completely different.

As soon as two people sit down to talk, learn to listen to the other's emotional place, understand from what place the other person works, what emotions arise around the subject at hand, a bridge between people is suddenly possible.

But many times, in organizations and day-to-day activities, emotion is seen as an inhibitor, a barrier that can interfere with desired goals. But often the opposite is true: Once emotion is given place, progress can be made.

You, and the people around you at work, are going to make mistakes. Punishment and grudges, toward yourself or others, keep you shackled to the past. Be willing to let go of what happened so that you can create something better for the future. Remember this when work is tense or you are in some sort of conflict with a coworker, boss, or customer: There is a quiet place inside of you, a place kept safe for you, where truth and wisdom remain protected and unharmed and where you can hold these tensions. Choices are ever present in your work life, even when you may believe otherwise, and directing your thoughts to stillness and peace of mind is always one of them.

A few years ago I was called to help two start-up partners at an organization with about fifteen people. The partners, let's call them Sarah and David, had difficulty functioning together, and there was a lack of clear communication between them. Their individual and collective motivations were unclear, as was the company vision. Neither of their roles was defined—but that wasn't all. After several conversations with employees, I realized that there was an equally significant problem regarding a senior executive—a company vice president we'll call Simon. Simon was very professional and had extensive experience, but his interpersonal relationships were marked by aggression; as a result, attrition was high.

Simon also had a tendency to put himself between Sarah and David. It was classic triangulation. Triangulation occurs when a person attempts to control the flow, interpretation, and nuances of communication between two separate actors or groups of actors. Ensuring that communication flows through and constantly relates back to that individual gives him or her a feeling of importance. Simon took advantage of the partners' disagreement to further his own agenda. Because Sarah and David did not confront him and set boundaries, he followed his own path, even if it damaged the company and the rest of the employees.

I realized that Sarah and David were afraid of confronting Simon, so afraid of dealing with him that Simon was able to poison the corporate culture and the company. It was their job, however, to deal with the various tensions: the tension between the vice president and the employees, the tension between personal inconvenience to deal with Simon and the needs of the organization, and the tension between open and closed communication. In working with the partners, I outlined all of this. Many times in such situations, managers simply start looking for a replacement without confronting the current issue, but we talked about the impact of the broader picture as well as the implications of Simon's current conduct.

Sarah and David needed to acknowledge the unpleasant feelings of fear and discomfort, without letting those emotions manage them.

As Peter M. Senge, C. Otto Scharmer, Joseph Jaworski, and Betty Sue Flowers point out in their book *Presence*, presence is a deep listening, an openness beyond the personal and historical perception of the thinking person through the intellect or logic that allows the release of old identities and the formation of new knowledge.[1] Acting from a state of presence can allow the field of communication to change, and the forces that shape the situation can shift from a reproduction of the past to a state where a future emerges, is formed, and consequently fulfilled. According to Buddhism, this state of mind requires silence of mind; that is, emptying our mind of our thoughts, which may eliminate the boundaries between the self and others and allow self-transcendence.

Presence is also about accepting the paradox of not knowing all the answers and the nonlinearity of the process. Sometimes we do not know why a particular thing is happening. But in our not knowing everything all at once, new opportunities can be created. Sometimes a creative leap happens because it is precisely the ability to stay and be present that allows it; otherwise, we are so motivated by our goals that we can lose sight of opportunities along the way. Being in a position of openness and curiosity allows for newness.

You can wish all you want for something or someone in your work life to be different, but a better use of your time would be to see that peace of mind and success are obtained by practicing acceptance of what you cannot change and actively addressing what you can. The greatest energy depleter is your fear. The most powerful energizer is making room for creativity and working through the tension.

FEAR AND UNRAVELING

When things seem to be going from bad to worse in your work, remember this: Fear of tension is at the core of any conflict or upset, but we do not have to be afraid of it.

When we offer kindness and patience to ourselves and one another, tensions can be unraveled.

But mindfulness is not about *not* feeling fear. Mindfulness means being connected to an experience or emotion, and this can definitely include fear. However, this emotion must not manage us in a manner that would make us become paralyzed and avoid conflict, or switch to automatic behavior.

Your happiness, purpose, and success at work are dependent on recognizing and ceasing to play these games. Your negative emotions and judgments in regard to work are like well-baited hooks waiting for you to bite, and then be reeled in by your own fearful mind.

When a tiger sees a deer in front of it, its instinct is to attack in order to survive, while the deer instinctively runs for its life. Each of us has our own instinctive pattern, the most common being fight, freeze, flight. But unlike animals in the wild, we can increase our awareness and respond from a free choice and not solely based upon our instincts. Psychologists once thought that those of us who managed our lives the best were those who relied on unconscious reactions, what most of us would call "gut instinct." The reality, though, is that after decades of testing, psychologists found that following our gut instincts actually puts us at a massive *dis*advantage: In doing so, we choose the wrong job paths, the most unhealthy foods, and even poor relationships.[2] The same research has shown that the people who feel more content in life and achieve more of their goals are those who take a bit more of a circuitous path to making a decision. This doesn't mean that they spend a whole lot more *time* making that decision but that they have better decision-making tools, such as self-awareness, reflection, and adaptability.

As managers, fear prevents us from protecting the interests of our employees because we are used to pleasing others and avoiding conflict zones. This situation does not come from choice and mindful awareness but the opposite: In this situation, the emotion manages us instead of us managing it.

Fear is at the core of any conflict or upset, and fear is something your mind makes up. But the greatest changes at work come from changes you make in your own mind. Themes of fear and revenge can be switched to themes of letting go and moving on at any time you choose.

We can be inherently kind rather than giving into negative emotions. Often in our day-to-day stress, we get lost and forget we can direct our minds in this direction. Being lost, we become fearful and often find ourselves in endless cycles of attack and defense. To find the response that will bring you success, ask which is a more valuable use of your time at work: fueling fear or cultivating letting go and understanding.

At Sarah and David's company, it didn't take long for Simon to figure out that his role was not a good fit for him, especially once they began to set clearer boundaries and express their dissatisfaction and disapproval of his conduct. Their talks were held in a respectful and open manner, and a search was made for the right solution on both sides. Once things were laid on the table and openly and honestly examined, Simon decided to leave the company. But his termination was done in a respectful way that did no harm to the organization or his reputation.

After only a week, the right candidate arrived.

Being a mindful leader requires us to have the strength and courage to manage unpleasant emotions such as fear and discomfort, allowing us to act despite these feelings. Just as Brené Brown writes in her book *Dare to Lead*, integrity means choosing courage over comfort, which means being able to act according to our values and not just declare them.[3] It is worthwhile to dare and initiate a conversation in which we share uncomfortable feelings without being dragged to the opposite end, where anger and frustration dominate. More than that, we must take a position of openness to reality and allow the solution to emerge from the interaction and not vice versa.

We need to recognize with self-honesty when we are engaged in communication or a process at work that is not going well. It is important not to dig a deeper hole for yourself by continuing down the same road, typically thinking in the same ways, when that approach isn't bringing you what you want. Remember, progress on a path to mindfulness is nothing more than being able to believe there is another way to react, where previously you would have only listened to your fear and escalated in your upset.

STEP NINE: LEADING THROUGH TENSION

Dare to be present and vulnerable in meetings without knowing the solution in advance. The fearful part of your mind comes up with all sorts of crazy games it wants you to play.

- Respect, be open, and be mindful to other opinions, thoughts, and perspectives that arise during each interaction. If you are willing to be open-minded, what first appeared to be a problem or wrong in your workday can be transformed into a gift or a possible future opportunity. When you are anticipating conflict at work, ask your inner wisdom if there is a way to approach the situation without a posture of attack and defense. Asking for this kind of help is like seeing a storm coming and deciding to seek refuge instead of running directly into it.
- See people in your work who are attacking as fearful. This does not mean you have to agree with them, or let them take advantage of you; it does mean that you should not return the attack, which will only bring more your way.
- Create the time to look at a range of solutions rather than expecting one to be devised at the same meeting.
- Practice listening to yourself. Be attentive and connect to the different emotions that reside in you at every moment. Let them be; give them space without trying to change them. Just acknowledge them.

- Develop mindful awareness behavior: the ability to be connected to the experience of fear and discomfort; to stop, observe, accurately experience, and examine whether to act in spite of fear, or if our fear is a way of protecting ourselves from an action that is not good for us.
- Develop a curious and open mindset. Practice this state of mind during meetings and also with friends and family.
- Dare to be present in the unknown, always.

14

ENABLING FLOW

Water is fluid, soft, and yielding. But water will wear away rock, which is rigid and cannot yield. As a rule, whatever is fluid, soft, and yielding will overcome whatever is rigid and hard. This is another paradox: What is soft is strong.

—Lao Tzu

Each of us has certain abilities that are strengths.

From my youth, I always believed that everyone brings a gift when arriving into this world—a gift that is unique to that person alone. When each of us realizes that gift in the working world, we will succeed too. I have always thought that work should be like a game that encompasses a lot of joy, creativity, lightness, and great fun.

As a girl, I was an active participant in the Scout organization. I loved being a Scout from the bottom of my heart—the encounters with friends, the work and the values that came with it. I held various roles: apprentice, instructor, head of a battalion, and senior instructor.

Further down the road, as I searched for my professional path, the father of a close friend inspired me to explore organizational consulting. When I started my career as a consultant, I facilitated different workshops that allowed me to actually continue what I loved so much about being in Scouts: training, working with people, and so forth. Only now, I'm being paid for it.

When we do what we love out of passion and engagement, we enjoy it and are committed to it even when facing challenges. This is called flow.

Flow is a mental state of functioning in which a person is completely immersed in a sense of energy, focus, full engagement, and enjoyment of the creative process.

As noted by researcher Mihaly Csikszentmihalyi, flow is the creative process that can be triggered by trying to answer a problem that has no direct solution.[1] There is a subconscious force that brings hidden thoughts and ideas to the surface when there are no direct paths to success. This force can result in an abstraction of creativity to what can be achieved in the present moment alone, which Csikszentmihalyi suggests is the merging of action and awareness about one's creative process. At the same time, flow cannot be achieved without focusing on the ways in which different paths can be taken to reach the same end goal. Critical thinking is a way of training the brain to look at all possibilities, and to do so from a number of different points of view.

The more work is inherently similar to a game—with diverse, flexible, and appropriate challenges; clear goals; and instant feedback—the more enjoyable it will be, regardless of the employee's level of development. A flow experience contains a playful element of lightness, fun, and action. Enjoyment of work can increase the psychological well-being that results from personal growth and realization of the potential of the self, and can therefore evoke a sense of meaning and self-transcendence. A game also provides a space for spontaneous trial and error, allowing self-organization and the formation of new patterns beyond oneself.

This may be part of the reason that trends in the corporate world aim toward gamification, introducing game elements to the work routine to support a work environment that will contribute to learning. Organizations use gamification to improve efficiency and creativity, and to drive business results.

The challenge in today's workplace reality is to allow people to act with inner passion and motivation, to be in a mode of playfulness. A situation must be created in which they will be able to bring their gift and passion to their daily work. This does not mean that if I am in flow and enjoyment, I do not face challenges and difficulties. But at the core of the matter is a strong passion and engagement and an inner motivation that helps me cope with those challenges and move on.

CREATING THE ENVIRONMENT TO FIND AND SUPPORT FLOW

As managers, we want to enable employees to be in a flow experience as much as possible.

To do so, it is necessary to maintain the right balance between employees' capabilities and the opportunities created to develop them.

Suppose a new customer asks that we travel to their location and deliver a presentation in Swahili, and I have an employee who wants to develop globally and engage new customers. That worker has the ability to do that, and he is reasonably proficient in Swahili. For the employee, this is a good opportunity for growth and development within the organization and for self-realization. Presumably, this means there is a high chance that he will enjoy a flow experience.

Using the same example, say we instead select another employee who also wants to develop globally and engage new customers, but whose ability to communicate in Swahili is poor. This second employee is more likely to feel anxious, be unable to enjoy the experience, and he may not be able to deliver the presentation.

Enabling the development of employees helps them get to flow faster.

Research has shown that there are organizations that are excellent at what they do and strive for excellence, but very few organizations place an uncompromising emphasis on developing people.[2] While they recognize the importance of improving processes and companies, they are not encouraging the continuous growth and improvement of the people doing the work itself. The philosophy behind this concept is that there needs to be a realization of human potential alongside the realization of organizational potential.

Some cultures support the growth and development of their employees through evaluation processes that enable people to identify their strengths and weaknesses and then set themselves a goal to develop one or two dimensions. It's necessary to see where an employee is in terms of level of interest in order to connect to his or her intrinsic motivation. Is she satisfied with the job? Is he exhausted and wanting to explore new interests?

A deliberately developmental organization is one with a culture that promotes the growth of its employees, not just in terms of material benefits or work-life balance. The idea is that the company will do everything it can to help employees overcome their own barriers, overcome their blind spots, and see mistakes and weaknesses as a key opportunity for personal growth.

Accomplishing this requires three things:

1. The need for a developing community where all are committed to the growth of employees.
2. The ability to identify the gap between desired and exhausted capabilities of employees and to make time for practice that enables continuous learning.
3. Recognizing employees' developmental aspirations and helping them develop to the edge of their ability.

Let's go back to Scott Shute's experience at LinkedIn. He was vice president of international customer service operations but is now the head of Mindfulness and Compassion Programs. How did that happen?

"About three years ago," he says, "I started teaching meditation classes at work. I have practiced meditation from the age of thirteen and started teaching meditation at the age of nineteen. It has always been an interest and a significant part of my life. I taught some ad hoc classes, and there was interest. I felt in my heart, then, that it would be natural for me to take it further. I met with the person in charge of health and well-being at the organization and asked if he would support it. Later, I met with the vice president of Human Resources on another matter. I said I was going to head a meditation group and asked her opinion about it. She was sold, and asked me to update her on how it was working. I had no choice but to start.

"At the first meeting there was one person, and I was convinced he was just as terrified as I was. The fact that I had to report about it to other departments also made things difficult for me. I wondered if I could really do that. *Would it be okay? What will this mean for our brand? What will people think of me?* But the second time there were three people; the third time, five people arrived. A year ago I suggested a path forward to my CEO and my boss to do this full-time and support all seventeen thousand of our global employees with mindfulness and compassion programs."

Shute's experience illustrates how a company can allow an employee to grow and fulfill a passion, add value as a human being, and bring about continued growth for LinkedIn through the development of employees and the organization. This required him to overcome the fears he had as a teenager, to face concerns about how he would be accepted in his workplace and how it would affect the company's brand. He also had to face the challenges of dealing with the company's bureaucracy.

It is worthwhile to explore how employees who are passionate about their own ideas can increase or develop new areas needed by the organization. This requires being open-minded while at the same time allowing the organization and its employees to grow and develop.

FLOW IS POSITIVE

Before he retired as vice president of Quality at Verint Systems, Moshe Ekroni conducted beginner and advanced workshops on the subject of positive psychology for managers and employees, with the aim of increasing their personal and professional well-being as well as their commitment and performance at work. More than 150 employees successfully completed the workshops. Working with the development team, his results were productive and efficient, the atmosphere positive, and motivation increased over the course of this project. It was also up to the teams to use their strengths, their values, and what brings meaning to their lives.

Ekroni's approach is similar to that at Tantalus. There, the company also sought to provide employees with satisfaction and meaning through maintaining the tension between control, flow, and flexibility, and between the employee and the organization. Their management team used a differentiation and integration technique that enabled employees to express their personal capabilities in the organizational space through tailoring a job and role-shifting according to their needs, wishes, and benefits.

At the heart of these methods is positive psychology, which has been linked back to mindfulness through the work of Martin Seligman, who suggests that managers must focus on an individual's strengths so that they can feel happiness translated into positive emotions, commitment, and a sense of meaning. Both Seligman and Csikszentmihalyi suggest that psychological traits such as hope, self-determination, and spirituality may in fact allow both individuals and communities to become healthier, more tolerant, and more ethical societies.[3] There is hope for the future in creating an opportunity to build wisdom through knowledge of self and an underlying respect for others.

Research shows that there is a fine line between the various emotions we use to process information in the workplace.[4]

Happiness and anger are known as certainty emotions. Basically, people who are in one of these two states know exactly how they feel and are likely to make decisions quickly and with absolute certainty, whether or not they are the right decisions for them or others in either the short or the long term. Happiness and anger cause the decision maker to process less-relevant information, and therefore these decisions aren't ever going to be informed by logic. Having employees in a happy or angry state isn't optimal for companies.

Fear and hope are uncertainty emotions. Both of these emotions activate more detail-oriented processing in the brain, where many different options and shifts can be considered. But here's the kicker: Fear and stress can directly lead to a loss of higher-order cognitive functions for hours after every stressor is introduced. In other words, many different options may be on the table for people under strain, but their ability to choose one of them is not likely to end well, either for the individual or for the company they work for.

Out of all of the emotions left in the basket, the one that applies to best-case decision making is hope.

The goal is to move people toward hope through calmness rather than induce them to work through fear to get things done quickly. Hope and calmness will lead to fewer mistake-laden shifts, but this requires patience.

The objective of a positive psychology approach is, of course, to increase self-awareness in order to bring about a more positive viewpoint in work life and to achieve confidence and personal balance. This positive point of view is thought to provide resiliency against life's negative events and to develop the skills and attitudes necessary for positive outcomes in life. Specifically, results from cross-sectional and longitudinal research have shown "improved productivity at work, having more meaningful relationships and less health care uptake."[5] In other words, when people have a positive attitude and hope for the future, they are more likely to take care of themselves and the people around them, resulting in a strong physical and mental health support system that will provide a buffer against future challenges in life and ensure less stress over the long term.

This behavior allows the employee to bring his or her added value to the company.

There is a connection between the use of positive psychology practices and what organizational behavior specialists call "valued subjective experiences." What this means is that we all have the propensity for positive and negative life experiences, but when these are seen through the lens of a subjectively hopeful point of view, they can become learning processes rather than mere experiences. A hopeful person is one who can see the ways in which life experiences can lend themselves to new opportunities for personal growth rather than to challenging issues that need to be examined through stress and strain. To this end, hope is not only an idealistic point of view; it is also a tool that creates the means by which an individual can move forward to a new way of integrating a range of experiences with the emotion of happiness. This bodes well for companies because employees are intrinsically fulfilled in their work.

Mindful leadership offers a holistic view that embodies a great deal of flexibility for employees and also considers their personal needs. This allows for the creation of roles that will allow employees to stay in the company longer.

An example of positive flow is resident in Tantalus's Star Program, which maps out employees the company wants to keep and promote and those who currently represent a lack of alignment between their needs and those of the organization, as well as employees the organization wants to keep but are in danger of leaving. Gold stars are connected to employees with added value; red stars represent a risk of leaving, either employee- or manager-led. An employee with both red and gold stars is an area of focus for management.

At Tantalus they're aiming for a win-win. If the employee is more satisfied, the company earns more. The Star Program was created through self-organizing employees and is reviewed through ongoing communication among members of the management team. The latter confronts the existing tension between employee expectations and actual conduct, setting boundaries by coordinating expectations and marking places for improvement or looking for ways to challenge employees. The company wants to motivate employees so they can move forward and develop and, ultimately, find a state of flow that will benefit the organization's goals.

Being realistic means being aware of the individual's past performance. Consider a person who expects good things to happen. At first glance, this may seem like wishful thinking about events that are out of the person's control. In some cases, that might be true. But for someone who has a consistent history of good experiences, it seems reasonable to expect that good experiences will continue, just as we all expect the sun to continue to rise every morning.

STEP TEN: CREATING FLOW

In order to create an environment for flow, remember that acting with purpose, no matter how little, creates solutions and positive flow in both directions. Our ability to find positive solutions is limited only by the doors to opportunity we choose to keep shut. If you want to open a door to opportunity for employees and company alike, start by asking the following questions:

- Is the employee currently fulfilling their role expectations?
- What strengths and added value does the employee have?
- Has the employee exhausted their ability in the organization, or are there other parts and strengths they have not expressed yet but want to fulfill?
- What intrigues the employee at this point?
- Is there an organizational need and alignment between the new capabilities the employee wants to realize and the organization's needs?
- What role can you tailor for the employee to bring added value to the organization?
- What organizational mechanisms can support the employee's growth alongside the organizational growth that comes with it?
- What are new directions the company wants to grow in, and who is capable of fulfilling these tasks/jobs?
- Which processes and mechanisms can be achieved in a more fun and flexible way?
- Which rotations can we encourage between jobs and employees?
- What can we offer in the culture to support the growth of our employees?

- Are you rewarding employees for learning, developing, and innovation? If not, what can you offer that specifically refers to your needed criteria?
- How might you offer new and flexible models for the nature and composition of work, such as part-time or flex-time scenarios that are built to honor employee needs?

15

FREEDOM AND
THE FUTURE

The way to do is to be.

—Lao Tzu

Dealing with the complex reality we face at work requires a new, mind-ful leadership that depends not only on one person, leadership that is based on relationships created by a social process that takes place between people in more egalitarian and dynamic relationships.

We've noticed it happening: The future is all about connected systems, systems where your phone pushes ads based on your conversations, your money transactions can be tracked instantly across the globe, and you get ticketed automatically when you run that red light. On the positive side, with the information that governments glean from surveillance, it is possible to achieve such goals as urban planning, road infrastructure, social service generation, and other laudable objectives. The more we have access to digital information, the more surveillance is planned. Media theory suggests that there is an inexorable rise in surveillance as digital information becomes available to those in positions of power. Social controls are rising, and it doesn't feel good. Research in this field shows that even though we're no longer physically clocking in and out as much, we're still being watched at work—from our emails to our social media use to our use of systems to track our hours spent on each project. And it's killing our individualism.[1]

It's no wonder we don't believe that we have the freedom to be ourselves; we delve into character to survive, or at least to do the best we can in life. When we don't feel free is also when we stop telling one another stories about what's bothering us. We stop sharing our frustrations and our challenges. At work, especially, we can't make mistakes without having a discussion about it, even though mistakes are normal and, as I've said before, we learn so very deeply from failure. We're missing out on the freedom to be ourselves. We have to encourage one another to be authentic; we have to support people being their true selves, provide them with the safety to feel at home and present, and trust them in making decisions.

We must have freedom to feel as if we can be mindful in every moment.

Since mindful leadership is no longer based solely on external characteristics of role definition, hierarchy, and external authority, it requires us—leaders—to increase the set of social capabilities to promote good interpersonal relationships, to build trust and partnership, and to harness people from a deeper place that creates meaning and connection and motivates processes.

As I have argued throughout this book, in order to be able to engage and inspire people, we must be mindful to others, but first we must be mindful to ourselves. We must be able to manage our inner world, which includes thoughts, feelings, emotions, and managing mindfulness at any given moment. As executives, the more mindful we are, the more we will be able to manage and lead from a more mindful and accurate place.

When we, as managers, act from a place of mindfulness and listening, we can contain complex states of uncertainty and hold different tensions. One of the most important tensions a mindful leader has to deal with is that between doing and being. A mindful leader is a leader who can go beyond the day-to-day activities and connect both to the broader picture and to higher purpose. This means cultivating the ability to be in being, at presence, to listening, and to pausing alongside our doing.

We each have to be accountable for living our truth in our lives and at work. Being truly who we are and following our instinctual knowledge means being self-aware of how we bring value to the world, to our work, and, most importantly, to ourselves. The ability to stop ourselves—to be here and now—along with doing sometimes involves discomfort and uncertainty. But today more than ever, our ability to be in a state of discomfort requires us to foster a presence in the complex realities in which we operate.

WHY DO WE FEEL SO AFRAID, RIGHT HERE AND NOW?

There is more tension than ever before in our way.

Nick Bostrom, founder of the Martin Programme on the Impacts of Future Technology and founding director of the Future of Humanity Institute at Oxford University, says that right now our future is faced with more existential threats than it ever has in the past. Due to greenhouse gases, biotechnology and nanotechnology, artificial intelligence, and stockpiled nuclear weapons, humankind, as he put it almost twenty years ago, has been rapidly approaching a critical phase in its career.[2]

Economist Tim Jackson, author of *Prosperity without Growth*[3] and former economics commissioner for the UK government's Sustainable Development Commission, has suggested that the very foundation of our working world and global economy is flawed and will continue to degrade, leaving billions of people wondering what went wrong.

Jared Diamond, the Pulitzer Prize–winning author, geographer, and acclaimed anthropologist, tells us that there are whole countries that have collapsed as a result of their inability to adapt, in part based on their fixation on a fear of the future, so much so that changing conditions overwhelmed them.[4] We're also afraid of our own personal futures; right now we don't know whether our jobs will, in fact, be taken by robots.[5]

The worst part is that fear paralyzes us when we can't see a viable next step.[6] Our fear of the future is so paralyzing that researchers are coming up with new ways to measure it. One such measurement, the Dark Future scale, has been devised in the past year because prior to this assessment, we had no way of understanding just how much fear we embody in today's rapidly changing world.[7]

The Dark Future research shows us that human beings are actually oriented toward the future. It's always on our minds. And yet there is a lack of preparation for everything the future has to offer. That's because embedded in the human experience is how we've been thrown into a time and space with a gap out in front of us. Constantly disappearing horizons amount to moving targets that not only shift but also become visible and invisible. The future contains variables we're not privy to yet, and there's no playbook for it.

The fact that a person is faced with an ambiguous space is inextricably linked with some fear of it. People differ in the tendency to feel anxiety, and this fear is also situationally conditioned. A certain level of fear for the future mobilizes effort, gives vividness to our experiences, and enriches life. However, fear often makes functioning seriously difficult, especially in problematic and stressful situations. In addition, some people are predisposed to react with fear to a variety of life situations. It means that nothing is clear.

Leaning back on traditional leadership means we're not supporting our world, or our economy.

Every-person-for-themselves capitalism has dominated the global economy since the 1970s. This approach assumes that all citizens not only have equal abilities to contribute to the market, but also that there are no barriers in the way of their doing so. This is problematic at best—approaching the economy this way ignores the critical tensions the world needs to address between social and economic goals. At worst, it's going to make it impossible for real, sustained growth. Companies need to recognize just how tenuous this approach is to their businesses' sustainability. The reality is that if businesses continue to push toward a race to the bottom in which everyone, including their employees, is meant to fend for themselves, societal and economic polarization will increase, real wages will decrease, and populations will have less financial stability and disposable incomes with which to buy goods and services. It is not possible to create true shared value in which greater profitability is derived from driving down costs, which, given the percentage of costs usually attributed to human resources, almost always results in cutting down on roles, increasing responsibility and strain for existing employees, and decreasing standard wage and benefits increases over time.

THROUGH MINDFULNESS, HOWEVER, WE CAN STAY FOCUSED ON THE PRESENT MOMENT

Companies have to make mindful changes from within, including ensuring equity and opportunity for all stakeholders, so they can continue to move forward.

An example of this is the US-based Gravity Payments, whose CEO famously raised all employees' salaries to at least seventy thousand dollars per year in recognition of the need for a living wage in the expensive city of Seattle—and, as a result, made more profit than ever expected. Companies can shift toward a new business model that allows them to recognize their responsibilities and make different choices that build capacity for all stakeholders, and away from a business model that is unethical and, in reality, uncompetitive in the new world of work. Mindfulness can provide the key to our next steps.

We have to support the freedom to explore our potential for self-awareness in life and, by extension, in the workplace. Really knowing who we are, rather than what character we're playing, leads to trusting ourselves and trusting our shifts so that we follow through on them. This begins with the ability to understand that we can conceive solutions that are authentically human, that are free from constraints and limitations. It is the only way we can begin to trust our intuition and know when we can be intentional about making decisions that are authentic—decisions that will serve us because we are fully aware of why we are doing something in the first place. Living with intention improves the quality of information used to make a decision. It reduces confirmation bias and overconfidence, allowing decision makers to better differentiate between relevant and irrelevant information. It reduces reliance on stereotypes and poor pattern detection. It helps employees appreciate uncertainty and deal with it productively. It facilitates the resolution of trade-offs, increasing the positive impact of collaboration and reducing procrastination. It ensures that employees are more open to feedback and less likely to misinterpret it. Living with intention means that employees will be less prone to making self-serving decisions and more prone to making company-serving decisions.

We fail to remember that there is the thing we're worried about, or the thing we're excited about, and then there is the story we tell ourselves about it. We have to be allowed to learn to peel away the layers not just of character but also of "culture" and the real-life chaos that is embedded in the modern workplace, the place where we spend most of our time and energy. We can create space for human stories and meaning, as well as curiosity and the opportunity for all of us to apply what we discover. Confidence, optimism, and personal experience can help us feel able to seek out information if and when we need it. Conflict, ambiguity, or uncertainty can have the opposite effect; people will stick to what they know rather than try something new unless they are able to master the art of being in the present moment and moving toward new wisdom, from within and from the connections they forge with their teams.

We will not have to avoid the experience of discomfort. The ability, through mindfulness, to enable paradoxes and dialectical tensions makes room for variability, dynamism, and personal and organizational growth.

New solutions can be produced and creative ideas be formed when we are able to hold tension together with action, to stop ourselves and pause for a moment.

ANOTHER NEW START FOR TANTALUS

Sustainability had more than one meaning at Tantalus.

A year after the failed bicycle initiative, Tantalus's Green Committee decided to promote an awareness activity about the environment, but this time the company did things differently. They sent a survey to employees asking what their preferences were. The company decided to break the Guinness world record for team floating in the Dead Sea, not only to achieve a goal as a group but also to raise public awareness about the plight of the Dead Sea, which is drying up due to climate change, compromising the needs of future generations. But the company's real growth came through deep listening, openness, and reflection, and the transformation of their personal and organizational identities. This was, to Tantalus, meaningful action that reflected the essence of what mattered to the team.

The more we act out of being present and from a fuller connection to ourselves, our emotions, and our feelings, the more we can be mindful to one another and create better relationships based on empathy and compassion that creates a sense of belonging and community. As we act with greater regard for ourselves, our employees, and the environment, we can be mindful to what is needed right now.

What is successful to each of us is connected to the meaning we take from our actions. It is connected to how we feel we can take over, can own the room in a certain space, whether it be an arena, a boardroom, or a living room. Are the people who have stopped chasing their dreams the ones who have reached success or happiness? Do they find it unattainable? Perhaps. Are they afraid of feeling successful? Maybe. Success, arguably, comes from contentment. It's the feeling that something has been achieved, that it has been underlined. That it requires no more activities. Success is like finally exhaling after holding our breath for a very long time.

Freedom also requires practice. Mindfulness starts from a lack of bias about what we're supposed to do and who we're supposed to be. It comes from calmness and psychological safety. It requests us to be real about who we are and what is important to us. From this place we can adopt our own identities, ones that resonate with us, so that there are no artificial barriers, no false characters, no expectations to play up to.

What does this look like? See your own metaphorical reflection. Are you a person people go to when they're facing a challenge? If the answer isn't yes, know that building your employee community or family or friend group starts with the mirror. Are you a person you would want to work for? Reflect on the hard truth of who you are, and who you want to be. It's okay if you're not there yet. It's okay to make a mistake. But it isn't okay to regret. Where we are right now is a result of the decisions and shifts we've made that got us here. Today is a new opportunity to shift again. After all, today is all we have. Right now is all we have. Right now is exactly where we need to be. Right now is our inflection point if we want it to be. It can be in the gutter or off the rails—we can choose.

Use your heart before your head. We love a good statistic and a set of rules, but this kind of thinking is getting us nowhere when it comes to connecting with others and building a future by our design only. Pretend there are no rules. What would you really say to someone who hurt you? Someone you admire? What would you say to yourself about what you need every day to feel comfortable enough to get your work done? What is the most intimate thing you'd be comfortable sharing now? What is the smallest intimacy you will allow for yourself? Do that.

Be real at work and at home. Give people trust, time, full attention, personalized rewards, and authentic thanks every day. Shift, learn, grow, discover. Allow yourself the freedom to be you. Make time to talk with people. When we give time and space to people, we give them time to discover what they mean. When they know exactly what they mean, it becomes easier to say it.

Be accountable and take ownership. When something goes wrong, or when you don't understand what's at stake or even what's happening, check yourself first. Be proactively transparent about when you're not perfect. This allows others to not be perfect too so that instead of hiding mistakes, we own up to them and move on.

Self-awareness is just this: We need to take the thoughts we have. See them through these four practices every day. Then challenge ourselves to go deeper into why we think the way we do; why we have biases; where our egos, rather than our hearts, our human selves, cause us to act. Doing this when we're troubled allows us to let those thoughts go, to get rid of negative intrusions on our days, saving us from ever having those thoughts again.

Success is an outcome. But it's no longer the end of the story. Self-awareness allows us to be mindful because it allows us to practice in a way that is fundamentally adaptable, cutting out the noise of everything else.

Every time we take a step toward mindfulness, we have the opportunity to change.

We know that *now* is the process.

NOTES

CHAPTER 1

1. Megan Brenan, "Nurses Keep Healthy Lead as Most Honest, Ethical Profession," *Gallup* (January 14, 2021), https://news.gallup.com/poll/224639/nurses-keep-healthy-lead-honest-ethical-profession.aspx.

2. Carter McNamara, "Overview of Cynicism in Business Organizations, Ethical Profession," *Management Help* (n.d.), https://managementhelp.org/personalwellness/cynicism/index.htm.

3. Omar Durrah, Monica Chaudhary, and Moaz Gharib, "Organizational Cynicism and Its Impact on Organizational Pride in Industrial Organizations," *International Journal of Environmental Research and Public Health* 16, no. 7 (2019): 1203.

4. Armi Mustosmäki, "The Intensification of Work," *Family, Work and Well-Being* (Springer, Cham, 2018): 77–90.

5. Ibid.

6. Microsoft Corporation, "The Next Great Disruption Is Hybrid Work—Are We Ready?" (2021 Work Trend Index: Annual Report, March 22, 2021).

7. Bessel A. Van der Kolk and Alexander C. McFarlane, eds., *Traumatic Stress: The Effects of Overwhelming Experience on Mind, Body, and Society*, second edition (Guilford Press, 2012).

8. Samma Faiz Rasool et al., "Sustainable Work Performance: The Roles of Workplace Violence and Occupational Stress," *International Journal of Environmental Research and Public Health* 17, no. 3 (2020): 912.

9. Ruth Q. Wolever et al., "Effective and Viable Mind-Body Stress Reduction in the Workplace: A Randomized Controlled Trial," *Journal of Occupational Health Psychology* 17, no. 2 (2012): 246.

10. Jon Kabat-Zinn, *Wherever You Go, There You Are: Mindfulness Meditation in Everyday Life* (Hyperion Books, 1994).

CHAPTER 2

1. Cheryl Jones (executive at Aetna) in discussion with the author, April 2019.

2. Richard Fernandez (CEO of SILYI) in discussion with the author, May 2019.

3. Sun Tzu, *Sun Tzu Art of War* (Vij Books, 2012).

4. Simon Linacre, "Time Well Spent? Differing Perceptions of Breaks at Work," *Human Resource Management International Digest* (2016).

5. Clive R. Boddy, "Corporate Psychopaths: Uncaring Citizens, Irresponsible Leaders," *Journal of Corporate Citizenship* 49 (2013): 8–16.

6. Reuters, "HSBC's Money Laundering Fines to Top US$1.5 Billion, Criminal Charges Likely" (November 5, 2012), https://financialpost.com/news/fp-street/hsbcs-money-laundering-fines-to-top-us1-5-billion-criminal-charges-likely.

7. Oli R. Mihalache et al., "Top Management Team Shared Leadership and Organizational Ambidexterity: A Moderated Mediation Framework," *Strategic Entrepreneurship Journal* 8, no. 2 (2014): 128–48.

8. Byungjoo Paek and Heesang Lee, "Strategic Entrepreneurship and Competitive Advantage of Established Firms: Evidence from the Digital TV Industry," *International Entrepreneurship and Management Journal* 14, no. 4 (2018): 883–925.

9. Iain Munro and Torkild Thanem, "The Ethics of Affective Leadership: Organizing Good Encounters without Leaders," *Business Ethics Quarterly* 28, no. 1 (2018): 51–69.

10. Huma Sarwar et al., "Ethical Leadership, Work Engagement, Employees' Well-Being, and Performance: A Cross-Cultural Comparison," *Journal of Sustainable Tourism* 28, no. 12 (2020): 2008–26.

11. Changsuk Ko et al., "Ethical Leadership: An Integrative Review and Future Research Agenda," *Ethics & Behavior* 28, no. 2 (2018): 104–32.

12. Scott B. Dust et al., "Ethical Leadership and Employee Success: Examining the Roles of Psychological Empowerment and Emotional Exhaustion," *The Leadership Quarterly* 29, no. 5 (2018): 570–83; Gary M. Fleischman et al., "Ethics Versus Outcomes: Managerial Responses to Incentive-Driven and Goal-Induced Employee Behavior," *Journal of Business Ethics* 158, no. 4 (2019): 951–67.

13. Stephen R. Barley and Gideon Kunda, "Design and Devotion: Surges of Rational and Normative Ideologies of Control in Managerial Discourse," *Administrative Science Quarterly* (1992): 363–99.

14. Etienne Wenger, *Communities of Practice: Learning, Meaning and Identity* (Cambridge, England: Cambridge University Press, 1998).

CHAPTER 3

1. Adam Moore and Peter Malinowski, "Meditation, Mindfulness and Cognitive Flexibility," *Consciousness and Cognition* 18, no. 1 (2009): 176–86.

2. Richard Chambers, Barbara Chuen Yee Lo, and Nicholas B. Allen, "The Impact of Intensive Mindfulness Training on Attentional Control, Cognitive Style, and Affect," *Cognitive Therapy and Research* 32, no. 3 (2008): 303–22.

3. Stefan G. Hofmann et al., "The Effect of Mindfulness-Based Therapy on Anxiety and Depression: A Meta-Analytic Review," *Journal of Consulting and Clinical Psychology* 78, no. 2 (2010): 169.

4. Norman A. S. Farb et al., "Minding One's Emotions: Mindfulness Training Alters the Neural Expression of Sadness," *Emotion* 10, no. 1 (2010): 25.

5. Mathias Dekeyser et al., "Mindfulness Skills and Interpersonal Behaviour," *Personality and Individual Differences* 44, no. 5 (2008): 1235–45.

CHAPTER 4

1. Robert Greenleaf, *The Power of Servant Leadership* (San Francisco: Berrett-Koehler, 2002).

CHAPTER 5

1. Robert Greenleaf, *The Power of Servant Leadership* (San Francisco: Berrett-Koehler, 2002): 31.

2. "Business Roundtable Redefines the Purpose of a Corporation to Promote 'An Economy That Serves All Americans,'" *Business Roundtable* (August 19, 2019), www.businessroundtable.org/business-roundtable-redefines-the-purpose-of-a-corporation-to-promote-an-economy-that-serves-all-americans.

CHAPTER 6

1. Sara W. Lazar et al., "Meditation Experience Is Associated with Increased Cortical Thickness," *Neuroreport* 16, no. 17 (2005): 1893.

2. Brendan D. Kelly, "Buddhist Psychology, Psychotherapy and the Brain: A Critical Introduction," *Transcultural Psychiatry* 45, no. 1 (2008): 5–30.

3. Fadel Zeidan et al., "Mindfulness Meditation Improves Cognition: Evidence of Brief Mental Training," *Consciousness and Cognition* 19, no. 2 (2010): 597–605.

4. Nurper Gökhan, Edward F. Meehan, and Kevin Peters, "The Value of Mindfulness-Based Methods in Teaching at a Clinical Field Placement," *Psychological Reports* 106, no. 2 (2010): 455–66.

5. Samuel Knapp, Michael C. Gottlieb, and Mitchell M. Handelsman, "Enhancing Professionalism through Self-Reflection," *Professional Psychology: Research and Practice* 48, no. 3 (2017): 167–74.

6. C. Dominik Guess, Sarah J. Donovan, and Dag Naslund, "Improving Dynamic Decision Making through Training and Self-Reflection," *Judgment and Decision Making* 10, no. 4 (2015): 284–95.

7. Miles M. Yang, Yucheng Zhang, and Feifei Yang, "How a Reflection Intervention Improves the Effect of Learning Goals on Performance Outcomes in a Complex Decision-Making Task," *Journal of Business and Psychology* 33, no. 5 (2018): 579–93.

8. Jane So et al., "The Psychology of Appraisal: Specific Emotions and Decision-Making," *Journal of Consumer Psychology* 25, no. 3 (2015): 359–71.

9. Ruth Helyer, "Learning through Reflection: The Critical Role of Reflection in Work-Based Learning (WBL)," *Journal of Work-Applied Management* 7, no. 1 (2015): 15–27.

10. Carol S. Dweck, *Mindset: The New Psychology of Success* (Random House, 2008).

11. Satya Nadella, *Hit Refresh* (Bentang Pustaka, 2018).

CHAPTER 7

1. David Bohm, *Unfolding Meaning: A Weekend of Dialogue* (Routledge, 1985).

2. Albert Mehrabian, "Inference of Attitudes from the Posture, Orientation, and Distance of a Communicator," *Journal of Consulting and Clinical Psychology* 32, no. 3 (1968): 296.

CHAPTER 8

1. Daniel Goleman, *Emotional Intelligence* (Wiley, 2012).

CHAPTER 9

1. Charles Duhigg, "What Google Learned from Its Quest to Build the Perfect Team," *The New York Times Magazine* 26 (2016).
2. Patricia Shaw, *Changing Conversations in Organizations: A Complexity Approach to Change* (Routledge, 2003).
3. Amy C. Edmondson, *The Fearless Organization: Creating Psychological Safety in the Workplace for Learning, Innovation, and Growth* (John Wiley & Sons, 2018).
4. Duhigg, op. cit.
5. Y. Orbach, "A Group of Self-Compassion: Practices for Broadening Self-Compassion in Israel," *Israeli Magazine for Facilitation and Group Therapy* 23, no. 1 (2008).

CHAPTER 10

1. Susan Gillis Chapman, *The Five Keys to Mindful Communication: Using Deep Listening and Mindful Speech to Strengthen Relationships, Heal Conflicts, and Accomplish Your Goals* (Shambhala Publications, 2012).
2. Janice Marturano, *Finding the Space to Lead: A Practical Guide to Mindful Leadership* (Bloomsbury Publishing USA, 2014).
3. Dan Ariely, *A Taste of Irrationality: Predictably Irrational and Upside of Irrationality* (HarperCollins, 2010).
4. Carey K. Morewedge et al., "Debiasing Decisions: Improved Decision Making with a Single Training Intervention," *Policy Insights from the Behavioral and Brain Sciences* 2, no. 1 (2015): 129–40.
5. Alexandre A. Bachkirov, "Managerial Decision Making under Specific Emotions," *Journal of Managerial Psychology* 30, no. 7 (2015): 861–74.
6. Deniz Vatansever, David K. Menon, and Emmanuel A. Stamatakis, "Default Mode Contributions to Automated Information Processing," *Proceedings of the National Academy of Sciences* 114, no. 48 (2017): 12821–26.
7. Dante Mantini et al., "Default Mode of Brain Function in Monkeys," *Journal of Neuroscience* 31, no. 36 (2011): 12954–62.

8. Antoine Bechara et al., "Deciding Advantageously before Knowing the Advantageous Strategy," *Science* 275, no. 5304 (1997): 1293–95.

CHAPTER 11

1. Peter J. Fadde and Gary A. Klein, "Deliberate Performance: Accelerating Expertise in Natural Settings," *Performance Improvement* 49, no. 9 (2010): 5–14.

CHAPTER 12

1. Michael Taft, "Is Mindfulness the Ultimate Business Skill?" *Wisdom Labs* (May 19, 2017), https://blog.wisdomlabs.com/blog/mindfulness-ultimate-business-skill.
2. Peter Fleming and Andrew Sturdy, "'Just Be Yourself!': Towards Neo-Normative Control in Organisations," *Employee Relations* 31, no. 6 (2009): 569–83.

CHAPTER 13

1. Peter M. Senge et al., *Presence: An Exploration of Profound Change in People, Organizations, and Society* (Currency, 2005).
2. Mark R. Nieuwenstein et al., "On Making the Right Choice: A Meta-Analysis and Large-Scale Replication Attempt of the Unconscious Thought Advantage," *Judgment and Decision Making* 10, no. 1 (2015): 1–17.
3. Brené Brown, *Dare to Lead: Brave Work. Tough Conversations. Whole Hearts* (Random House, 2018).

CHAPTER 14

1. Mihaly Csikszentmihalyi, *Society, Culture, and Person: A Systems View of Creativity* (Springer Netherlands, 2014).
2. Robert Kegan and Lisa Laskow Lahey, *An Everyone Culture: Becoming a Deliberately Developmental Organization* (Harvard Business Review Press, 2016).

3. Martin E. P. Seligman and Mihaly Csikszentmihalyi, "Positive Psychology: An Introduction," *Flow and the Foundations of Positive Psychology* (Springer, 2014): 279–98.

4. So et al., op. cit.

5. Linda Bolier et al., "Positive Psychology Interventions: A Meta-Analysis of Randomized Controlled Studies," *BMC Public Health* 13, no. 1 (2013): 1–20.

CHAPTER 15

1. Norbert Ebert, *Individualisation at Work: The Self between Freedom and Social Pathologies* (Routledge, 2016).

2. Nick Bostrom, "Existential Risks: Analyzing Human Extinction Scenarios and Related Hazards," *Journal of Evolution and Technology* 9 (2002).

3. Tim Jackson, *Prosperity without Growth: Foundations for the Economy of Tomorrow* (Taylor & Francis, 2016).

4. Jared Diamond, *Collapse: How Societies Choose to Fail or Survive* (Viking, 2005).

5. David A. Spencer, "Fear and Hope in an Age of Mass Automation: Debating the Future of Work," *New Technology, Work and Employment* 33, no. 1 (2018): 1–12.

6. Peter Newman, Timothy Beatley, and Heather Boyer, *Resilient Cities: Responding to Peak Oil and Climate Change* (Island Press, 2009).

7. Zbigniew Zaleski et al., "Development and Validation of the Dark Future Scale," *Time & Society* 28, no. 1 (2019): 107–23.

BIBLIOGRAPHY

Ariely, Dan. *A Taste of Irrationality: Predictably Irrational and Upside of Irrationality.* HarperCollins, 2010.

Bachkirov, Alexandre A. "Managerial Decision Making under Specific Emotions." In *Journal of Managerial Psychology* 30, no. 7 (2015): 861–74.

Barley, Stephen R., and Gideon Kunda. "Design and Devotion: Surges of Rational and Normative Ideologies of Control in Managerial Discourse." In *Administrative Science Quarterly* (1992): 363–99.

Bechara, Antoine, et al. "Deciding Advantageously before Knowing the Advantageous Strategy." In *Science* 275, no. 5304 (1997): 1293–95.

Boddy, Clive R. "Corporate Psychopaths: Uncaring Citizens, Irresponsible Leaders." In *Journal of Corporate Citizenship* 49 (2013): 8–16.

Bohm, David. *Unfolding Meaning: A Weekend of Dialogue.* Routledge, 1985.

Bolier, Linda, et al. "Positive Psychology Interventions: A Meta-Analysis of Randomized Controlled Studies." In *BMC Public Health* 13, no. 1 (2013): 1 20.

Bostrom, Nick. "Existential Risks: Analyzing Human Extinction Scenarios and Related Hazards." In *Journal of Evolution and Technology* 9 (2002).

Brenan, Megan. "Nurses Keep Healthy Lead as Most Honest, Ethical Profession." In *Gallup*, January 14, 2021. https://news.gallup.com/poll/224639/nurses-keep-healthy-lead-honest-ethical-profession.aspx.

Brown, Brené. *Dare to Lead: Brave Work. Tough Conversations. Whole Hearts.* Random House, 2018.

"Business Roundtable Redefines the Purpose of a Corporation to Promote 'An Economy That Serves All Americans.'" In *Business Roundtable,* August 19,

2019. www.businessroundtable.org/business-roundtable-redefines-the-purpose -of-a-corporation-to-promote-an-economy-that-serves-all-americans.

Chambers, Richard, Barbara Chuen Yee Lo, and Nicholas B. Allen. "The Impact of Intensive Mindfulness Training on Attentional Control, Cognitive Style, and Affect." In *Cognitive Therapy and Research* 32, no. 3 (2008): 303–22.

Csikszentmihalyi, Mihaly. *Society, Culture, and Person: A Systems View of Creativity.* Springer Netherlands, 2014.

Dekeyser, Mathias, et al. "Mindfulness Skills and Interpersonal Behaviour." In *Personality and Individual Differences* 44, no. 5 (2008): 1235–45.

Diamond, Jared. *Collapse: How Societies Choose to Fail or Survive.* Viking, 2005.

Duhigg, Charles. "What Google Learned from Its Quest to Build the Perfect Team." In *The New York Times Magazine*, 26, 2016.

Durrah, Omar, Monica Chaudhary, and Moaz Gharib. "Organizational Cynicism and Its Impact on Organizational Pride in Industrial Organizations." In *International Journal of Environmental Research and Public Health* 16, no. 7 (2019): 1203.

Dust, Scott B., et al. "Ethical Leadership and Employee Success: Examining the Roles of Psychological Empowerment and Emotional Exhaustion." In *The Leadership Quarterly* 29, no. 5 (2018): 570–83.

Dweck, Carol S. *Mindset: The New Psychology of Success.* Random House, 2008.

Ebert, Norbert. *Individualisation at Work: The Self Between Freedom and Social Pathologies.* Routledge, 2016.

Edmondson, Amy C. *The Fearless Organization: Creating Psychological Safety in the Workplace for Learning, Innovation, and Growth.* John Wiley & Sons, 2018.

Fadde, Peter J., and Gary A. Klein. "Deliberate Performance: Accelerating Expertise in Natural Settings." In *Performance Improvement* 49, no. 9 (2010): 5-14.

Farb, Norman A. S., et al. "Minding One's Emotions: Mindfulness Training Alters the Neural Expression of Sadness." In *Emotion* 10, no. 1 (2010): 25.

Fleischman, Gary M., et al. "Ethics versus Outcomes: Managerial Responses to Incentive-Driven and Goal-Induced Employee Behavior." In *Journal of Business Ethics* 158, no. 4 (2019): 951-67.

Fleming, Peter, and Andrew Sturdy. "'Just Be Yourself!': Towards Neo-normative Control in Organisations." In *Employee Relations* 31, no. 6 (2009): 569-83.

Gökhan, Nurper, Edward F. Meehan, and Kevin Peters. "The Value of Mindfulness-Based Methods in Teaching at a Clinical Field Placement." In *Psychological Reports* 106, no. 2 (2010): 455-66.

Goleman, Daniel. *Emotional Intelligence.* Wiley, 2012.

Greenleaf, Robert. *The Power of Servant Leadership.* San Francisco: Berrett-Koehler, 2002.

Guess, C. Dominik, Sarah J. Donovan, and Dag Naslund. "Improving Dynamic Decision Making through Training and Self-Reflection." In *Judgment and Decision Making* 10, no. 4 (2015): 284–95.

Helyer, Ruth. "Learning through Reflection: The Critical Role of Reflection in Work-Based Learning (WBL)." In *Journal of Work-Applied Management* 7, no. 1 (2015): 15–27.

Hofmann, Stefan G., et al. "The Effect of Mindfulness-Based Therapy on Anxiety and Depression: A Meta-Analytic Review." In *Journal of Consulting and Clinical Psychology* 78, no. 2 (2010): 169.

Jackson, Tim. *Prosperity without Growth: Foundations for the Economy of Tomorrow.* Taylor & Francis, 2016.

Kabat-Zinn, Jon. *Wherever You Go, There You Are: Mindfulness Meditation in Everyday Life.* Hyperion Books, 1994.

Kegan, Robert, and Lisa Laskow Lahey. *An Everyone Culture: Becoming a Deliberately Developmental Organization.* Harvard Business Review Press, 2016.

Kelly, Brendan D. "Buddhist Psychology, Psychotherapy and the Brain: A Critical Introduction." In *Transcultural Psychiatry* 45, no. 1 (2008): 5–30.

Knapp, Samuel, Michael C. Gottlieb, and Mitchell M. Handelsman. "Enhancing Professionalism through Self-Reflection." In *Professional Psychology: Research and Practice* 48, no. 3 (2017): 167–74.

Ko, Changsuk, et al. "Ethical Leadership: An Integrative Review and Future Research Agenda." In *Ethics & Behavior* 28, no. 2 (2018): 104–32.

Lazar, Sara W., et al. "Meditation Experience Is Associated with Increased Cortical Thickness." In *Neuroreport* 16, no. 17 (2005): 1893.

Linacre, Simon. "Time Well Spent? Differing Perceptions of Breaks at Work." In *Human Resource Management International Digest* (2016).

Mantini, Dante, et al. "Default Mode of Brain Function in Monkeys." In *Journal of Neuroscience* 31, no. 36 (2011): 12954–62.

Marturano, Janice. *Finding the Space to Lead: A Practical Guide to Mindful Leadership.* Bloomsbury Publishing USA, 2014.

McNamara, Carter. "Overview of Cynicism in Business Organizations, Ethical Profession." In *Management Help* (n.d.). https://managementhelp.org/personalwellness/cynicism/index.htm.

Mehrabian, Albert. "Inference of Attitudes from the Posture, Orientation, and Distance of a Communicator." In *Journal of Consulting and Clinical Psychology* 32, no. 3 (1968): 296.

Microsoft Corporation. "The Next Great Disruption Is Hybrid Work—Are We Ready?" 2021 Work Trend Index: Annual Report, March 22, 2021.

Mihalache, Oli R., et al. "Top Management Team Shared Leadership and Organizational Ambidexterity: A Moderated Mediation Framework." In *Strategic Entrepreneurship Journal* 8, no. 2 (2014): 128–48.

Moore, Adam, and Peter Malinowski. "Meditation, Mindfulness and Cognitive Flexibility." In *Consciousness and Cognition* 18, no. 1 (2009): 176–86.

Morewedge, Carey K., et al. "Debiasing Decisions: Improved Decision Making with a Single Training Intervention." In *Policy Insights from the Behavioral and Brain Sciences* 2, no. 1 (2015): 129–40.

Munro, Iain, and Torkild Thanem. "The Ethics of Affective Leadership: Organizing Good Encounters without Leaders." In *Business Ethics Quarterly* 28, no. 1 (2018): 51–69.

Mustosmäki, Armi. "The Intensification of Work." In *Family, Work and Well-Being*. Springer, Cham, 2018: 77–90.

Nadella, Satya. *Hit Refresh*. Bentang Pustaka, 2018.

Newman, Peter, Timothy Beatley, and Heather Boyer. *Resilient Cities: Responding to Peak Oil and Climate Change*. Island Press, 2009.

Nieuwenstein, Mark R., et al. "On Making the Right Choice: A Meta-Analysis and Large-Scale Replication Attempt of the Unconscious Thought Advantage." In *Judgment and Decision Making* 10, no. 1 (2015): 1–17.

Orbach, Y. "A Group of Self-Compassion: Practices for Broadening Self-Compassion in Israel." In *Israeli Magazine for Facilitation and Group Therapy*, 23, no. 1 (2008).

Paek, Byungjoo, and Heesang Lee. "Strategic Entrepreneurship and Competitive Advantage of Established Firms: Evidence from the Digital TV Industry." In *International Entrepreneurship and Management Journal* 14, no. 4 (2018): 883–925.

Rasool, Samma Faiz, et al. "Sustainable Work Performance: The Roles of Workplace Violence and Occupational Stress." In *International Journal of Environmental Research and Public Health* 17, no. 3 (2020): 912.

Sarwar, Huma, et al. "Ethical Leadership, Work Engagement, Employees' Well-Being, and Performance: A Cross-Cultural Comparison." In *Journal of Sustainable Tourism* 28, no. 12 (2020): 2008–26.

Seligman, Martin E. P., and Mihaly Csikszentmihalyi. "Positive Psychology: An Introduction." In *Flow and the Foundations of Positive Psychology*. Springer, 2014: 279–98.

Senge, Peter M., et al. *Presence: An Exploration of Profound Change in People, Organizations, and Society*. Currency, 2005.

Shaw, Patricia. *Changing Conversations in Organizations: A Complexity Approach to Change*. Routledge, 2003.

So, Jane, et al. "The Psychology of Appraisal: Specific Emotions and Decision-Making." In *Journal of Consumer Psychology* 25, no. 3 (2015): 359–71.

Spencer, David A. "Fear and Hope in an Age of Mass Automation: Debating the Future of Work." In *New Technology, Work and Employment* 33, no. 1 (2018): 1–12.

Taft, Michael. "Is Mindfulness the Ultimate Business Skill?" In *Wisdom Labs,* May 19, 2017. https://blog.wisdomlabs.com/blog/mindfulness-ultimate-business-skill.

Tzu, Sun. *Sun Tzu Art of War.* Vij Books, 2012.

Van der Kolk, Bessel A., and Alexander C. McFarlane, eds. *Traumatic Stress: The Effects of Overwhelming Experience on Mind, Body, and Society*, second edition. Guilford Press, 2012.

Vatansever, Deniz, David K. Menon, and Emmanuel A. Stamatakis. "Default Mode Contributions to Automated Information Processing." In *Proceedings of the National Academy of Sciences* 114, no. 48 (2017): 12821–26.

Wenger, Etienne. *Communities of Practice: Learning, Meaning and Identity.* Cambridge, England: Cambridge University Press, 1998.

Wolever, Ruth Q., et al. "Effective and Viable Mind-Body Stress Reduction in the Workplace: A Randomized Controlled Trial." In *Journal of Occupational Health Psychology* 17, no. 2 (2012): 246.

Yang, Miles M., Yucheng Zhang, and Feifei Yang. "How a Reflection Intervention Improves the Effect of Learning Goals on Performance Outcomes in a Complex Decision-Making Task." In *Journal of Business and Psychology* 33, no. 5 (2018): 579–93.

Zaleski, Zbigniew, et al. "Development and Validation of the Dark Future Scale." In *Time & Society* 28, no. 1 (2019): 107–23.

Zeidan, Fadel, et al. "Mindfulness Meditation Improves Cognition: Evidence of Brief Mental Training." In *Consciousness and Cognition* 19, no. 2 (2010): 597–605.

INDEX

ABOUT THE AUTHOR

Keren Tsuk, PhD, is a keynote speaker, consultant, and thought leader in twenty-first century leadership. Founder of the consulting firm Wisdom to Lead, Tsuk specializes in developing senior management teams and corporate leadership. She guides companies and senior management teams to reach their full potential using various techniques in the field of mindfulness. She has developed an innovative Mindfulness Based Leadership (MBL) course and retreat, which she conducts for organizations around the world. Her practice extends to assisting executives to discover their own inner wisdom and maximize their overall leadership potential—both in and out of the workplace. With more than twenty years of experience working with senior management in the areas of transition, growth, and development processes, Tsuk has worked with companies such as Check Point, Verint, Amdocs, Ex Libris, Google, and Siemens. As a keynote speaker on the topic of the relationship between mindfulness and leadership, she has lectured at conferences worldwide and has been invited to speak at universities around the world, instructing graduate business school courses at PolyU in Hong Kong and Lahav Executive Education at Tel Aviv University, as well as teaching executive education courses at IDC Herzliya.

CPSIA information can be obtained
at www.ICGtesting.com
Printed in the USA
BVHW030743111021
618493BV00008B/3

9 781538 156360